# It Is Written

a hundred-day journey through the book of Job,
using the rest of Scripture to light the way

By Bethany Armstrong

# • Copyright Information •

© 2020 Bethany Joy Armstrong
All Rights Reserved

ISBN: 9798699278930 (Print)
Independently published: 1st Edition

Printed in the United States of America

# • Preface •

It is my prayer that this study of Job helps each of us to know God better, draws us to love Him more, and leads us to trust Him completely. I also hope that this study helps equip us for the trials of life that will inevitably come our way and softens our hearts toward God when we reflect on pain we have already borne. His love endures.

I wrote this study during the global Covid-19 pandemic, amidst intense civil and political unrest in the U.S., while unprecedented wildfires raged through my home state of California. My beloved uncle continued to fight the ravages of ALS, and my dear friend with four young children began treatments for invasive cancer. *All of creation is groaning for redemption.* There are wars being waged in the heavenlies, of which we see only a glimpse.

Life overflows with goodness and beauty; it is also wrought with spiritual warfare and suffering of every kind. In peace and in pain, the character of God and the truth of His Word remain steadfast; our job is to trust God, press on, and suffer well—with Christ in us, our hope of glory, and His written Word our lifeline. *"Lord, to whom shall we go? You have the words of eternal life"* (John 16:68).

Using this study guide, we will access that precious lifeline of Scripture. This workbook is designed to complement a commentary on the book of Job written by Ray Stedman, entitled *Let God Be God*. Stedman's book is a rich resource all on its own; I actually enjoyed it so much that I found myself reading it three times before deciding to write this study guide. However, I wished for two things as I read *Let God Be God*: (1) to share Stedman's book with everyone I know! and (2) to work through an interactive Bible study on the book of Job—realizing what a treasure trove it is and how much it relates to the rest of Scripture.

My inability to find exactly what I was looking for in an existing study guide inspired me to write this one. I trust that God has led me in this process and believe that He will direct this study into just the right hands. The process of writing it was hugely beneficial for me, and I hope that *Someone Out There Somewhere* will be helped by it, too.

This study guide asks questions of application and brings in the whole counsel of Scripture to shed light on the topics at hand. Jesus Himself taught us to rely on the written Word of God: *"It is written..."* Job did not have that resource—but since we do, we will use it to illuminate what we read on our journey through Job.

We will do a lot of sifting in this study. Which of Job's words and his friends' comments are true, and which misrepresent reality? We will also keep in mind that the writers of the commentary and workbook are fallible and finite, so what we read should be filtered accordingly and compared always to the infallible, infinite Word of God. Ideally, this study will simply help us mine deeper into the gold standard of Scripture. God's Word is *"living and active"* (Hebrews 4:12); thus, my intent in this study was to minimize personal commentary and to bring instead a plethora of Scripture to the discussion of Job, fully believing that God's Word can—and will—speak for itself, by the power of the Holy Spirit.

This study is designed to take 100 days, with each day of study requiring about 30 minutes. Memory verses are paced so that every ten days of the study, a new verse is introduced. It may work well to convene with a small group once every two weeks, and in that two-week period to cover ten days' worth of material; that would amount to a 20-week study with 10 total meetings. Alternatively, small-group meetings could occur weekly, with five days of study discussed each week; this would be a 20-week study with 20 total meetings. Of course, the study can just as well be done independently, too. The material is designed for anyone who wants "straight-up Scripture"—whether women or men, new believers or those who have been Christians for many years—and can be gone through at any pace in any which way; it is simply a tool to be used however its wielder deems best. You may even choose to go through one day's worth of study in a week and end up studying Job for nearly two years! Wouldn't that be something?

By the end of this study, you will have memorized ten Bible verses and will have studied the entire book of Job. You will have explored a wide range of subjects, discovering what the scope of the Bible has to say about them—including the topics of suffering, spiritual warfare, godly speech, expectations of life, the character of God, the importance of healthy theology, beneficial skepticism, the perceived silence of God, God's never giving up on His children, and even simply how to be a good friend.

As you will note in the topical index, this study touches on well over 100 different topics about God and the Christian life; and to investigate these subjects, you will be digging into over 50 books of the Bible. You will either become good friends with your Bible app or will gain great proficiency at navigating the pages of Scripture!

I am fully convinced that not a minute we spend studying the Word of God is ever wasted. We *need* God, we need to *know* God, and *we need to know His Word*. May He bless each of us in this endeavor, and may this study equip us to persevere through life unshaken by helping us grow deep roots in the knowledge of Him who loves us—our God who will never waste our pain.

*"Grace to all who love our Lord Jesus Christ with an undying love"*—Ephesians 6:24.

*Bethany*

Bethany Armstrong
October 2020

# • Suggested 20-Week Schedule •

| Week | Lesson Numbers (Days) | Memory Verse |
|------|----------------------|--------------|
| 1 | 1–5 | Job 23:10 |
| 2 | 6–10 | |
| 3 | 11–15 | 1 John 4:4 |
| 4 | 16–20 | |
| 5 | 21–25 | Psalm 91:1–2 |
| 6 | 26–30 | |
| 7 | 31–35 | 1 Thessalonians 5:11 |
| 8 | 36–40 | |
| 9 | 41–45 | 2 Corinthians 1:3 |
| 10 | 46–50 | |
| 11 | 51–55 | 1 Peter 4:19 |
| 12 | 56–60 | |
| 13 | 61–65 | Psalm 23:4 |
| 14 | 66–70 | |
| 15 | 71–75 | Job 36:5 |
| 16 | 76–80 | |
| 17 | 81–85 | Isaiah 33:6 |
| 18 | 86–90 | |
| 19 | 91–95 | Job 42:2 |
| 20 | 96–100 | |

# • Verses to Memorize •

| Days | Reference | Verse |
|------|-----------|-------|
| 1–10 | Job 23:10 | *"He knows the way that I take; when He has tested me, I will come forth as gold."* |
| 11–20 | 1 John 4:4 (ESV) | *"He who is in you is greater than he who is in the world."* |
| 21–30 | Psalm 91:1–2 | *"Whoever dwells in the shelter of the Most High will rest in the shadow of the Almighty. I will say of the LORD, 'He is my refuge and my fortress, my God, in whom I trust.' "* |
| 31–40 | 1 Thessalonians 5:11 | *"Encourage one another and build each another up..."* |
| 41–50 | 2 Corinthians 1:3 | *"Praise be to the God and Father of our Lord Jesus Christ, the Father of compassion and the God of all comfort..."* |
| 51–60 | 1 Peter 4:19 | *"Those who suffer according to God's will should commit themselves to their faithful Creator and continue to do good."* |
| 61–70 | Psalm 23:4 (ESV) | *"Even though I walk through the valley of the shadow of death, I will fear no evil, for You are with me..."* |
| 71–80 | Job 36:5 (NLT) | *"God is mighty, but He does not despise anyone! He is mighty in both power and understanding."* |
| 81–90 | Isaiah 33:6 | *"He will be the sure foundation for your times..."* |
| 91–100 | Job 42:2 | *"I know that You can do all things; no purpose of Yours can be thwarted."* |

# • Journeying Through Job •

| | | | |
|---|---|---|---|
| Overview | Days 1–5 | Job 22 | Day 54 |
| Job 1 | Days 6–13 | Job 23 | Day 55 |
| Job 2 | Days 14–20 | Job 24 | Day 56 |
| Job 3 | Days 21–22 | Job 25 | Day 57 |
| Job 4 | Days 23–24 | Job 26 | Day 58 |
| Job 5 | Day 25 | Job 27 | Day 60 |
| Job 6 | Day 26 | Job 28 | Day 61 |
| Job 7 | Day 27 | Job 29 | Day 62 |
| Job 8 | Day 29 | Job 30 | Day 63 |
| Job 9 | Day 31 | Job 31 | Days 64–65 |
| Job 10 | Days 31–32 | Job 32 | Days 67–69 |
| Job 11 | Day 33 | Job 33 | Days 70–73 |
| Job 12 | Day 34 | Job 34 | Days 74–77 |
| Job 13 | Days 35–37 | Job 35 | Day 78 |
| Job 14 | Days 38–41 | Job 36 | Days 79–80 |
| Job 15 | Days 43–44 | Job 37 | Day 80 |
| Job 16 | Day 45 | Job 38 | Days 81–84 |
| Job 17 | Day 46 | Job 39 | Day 84 |
| Job 18 | Day 47 | Job 40 | Days 85–87 |
| Job 19 | Days 48–50 | Job 41 | Days 87–89 |
| Job 20 | Day 52 | Job 42 | Days 90–94 |
| Job 21 | Day 53 | Conclusion | Days 95–100 |

# • Topical Index •

| Topic | Day(s) |
|---|---|
| Afterlife | See "Heaven" |
| Angels | 24 |
| Anger | 67, 91 |
| Behemoth and Leviathan | 87, 89 |
| Belonging | 28 |
| Bereans | 25 |
| Born again | 72 |
| Boundaries | 11, 22, 78 |
| Brevity of life | 38 |
| Character of God | 20, 24, 51, 76, 83, 89, 92, 96, 100 |
|     Changelessness | 3 |
|     Comfort | 44 |
|     Emotions | 27, 78 |
|     Faithfulness | 2 |
|     Goodness | 39 |
|     Love | 12, 24, 31 |
|     Majesty | 37, 80 |
|     Mercy | 56, 91 |
|     Mystery | 12 |
|     Omnipotence | See "Power" |
|     Omnipresence | 5, 14, 77 |
|     Omniscience | 64, 77, 79 |
|     Patience | 73 |
|     Perfection | 76 |
|     Personal | 49 |
|     Potter | 17 |
|     Power | 31, 34, 58, 82, 90 |
|     Protection | 22 |

| | |
|---|---|
| Character of God, *continued* | |
|     Provider | 84 |
|     Silence | 32, 56 |
|     Sovereignty | 9 |
|     Speaking | 71 |
|     Strength | 12 |
|     Sufficiency | 100 |
|     Timing | 42, 56 |
| Complaining | 26 |
| Confidence in God | 49 |
| Creation/nature | 34, 81, 82, 84, 88 |
| Darkness | 21, 47, 55, 62 |
| Death | 5, 21, 22 |
| Delighting in God | 75 |
| Doubt | 10, 88 |
| Dreams and visions | 71 |
| Emotions | 52, 55, 90 |
| Empathy | 33 |
| Entitlement/expectations | 4, 6, 17, 19 |
| Envy | 53 |
| Faith | 5, 55, 92, 98 |
| False accusations | 54 |
| Family | 94 |
| Fear | 70, 96 |
| Feelings | See "Emotions" |
| Fighting sin | 60, 64 |
| Forgiveness | 40, 54, 93, 94 |
| Friends (Job's) | 23, 91, 93 |

| Glory | 85 |
| --- | --- |
| God | See "Character of God" |
| Grace | 13 |
| Grief | 21, 62 |
| Heaven/afterlife/eternity | 14, 22, 41, 50, 99 |
| Heavenly realms | See "Spiritual warfare" |
| Holy Spirit | 44, 93 |
| Hope | 23, 48, 50, 73 |
| Human nature | 53 |
| Humility | 43, 65, 86, 98 |
| Identity | 28, 47, 57, 72 |
| Intellect | See "Mind" |
| Intercessory prayer | 93 |
| Interpreting Scripture | 8, 25, 36 |
| Jealousy | See "Envy" |
| Jesus Christ | 23, 31, 36, 40, 49, 50, 54, 72, 92 |
| Judgment | 50 |
| Light | 21, 47, 82 |
| Mediator | See "Jesus Christ" |
| Mercy | 56 |
| Mind/intellect | 46, 52, 96 |
| Obedience | 79 |
| Pain | 14, 51, 71; also see "Suffering" |
| Perseverance | 58 |
| Perspective | 27 |
| Pessimism | 39, 48 |

| | |
|---|---|
| Pharisaism | 51 |
| Prayer | 37, 42, 61, 78, 93, 98 |
| Pride | 43 |
| Purpose in life | 97 |
| Purpose in suffering | 14, 21, 23, 29, 58, 79, 99 |
| Questioning | 1, 2, 24, 25, 29, 57, 66, 74, 75 |
| Relationships | 26, 30, 33, 35, 43–45, 48, 73, 93–95; also see "Speech" |
| Relative truth | 74 |
| Repentance | 66, 86 |
| Reputation | 62, 67 |
| Sacrifice | 92 |
| Saints | 59 |
| Sanctification | 32, 77 |
| Satan | 14, 44, 88; also see "Spiritual warfare" |
| Scripture | 1, 8, 15, 25, 36, 42, 46, 96 |
| Self-control | 67, 69 |
| Servanthood | 98; also see "Humility" |
| Silence of God | 32, 56 |
| Sin | 64, 66 |
| Speech | 4, 18, 19, 26, 29, 30, 33, 35, 45, 48, 52, 57, 69, 71 |
| Spiritual warfare | 3, 8–11, 16, 18, 24, 87, 88, 97 |
| Standing firm | 60 |
| Suffering | 1, 2, 5, 9, 11, 14, 20, 21, 23, 28, 29, 37, 39, 48–51, 58, 59, 78, 79, 99 |
| Testing | 9 |

| | |
|---|---|
| Theodicy | 12 |
| Theology | 24, 30, 32, 33 |
| Trusting God | 51, 55 |
| Will of God | 59 |
| Wisdom | 43, 47, 61, 68 |
| Worldly philosophy | 10, 19, 38, 41, 87, 97 |
| Worship | 13, 34, 98 |

# • Recommended Resources •

*This list is by no means exhaustive, but it includes a handful of helps in a few key areas.*

Bibles:

Study Bible: *The ESV Study Bible*

Parallel Bible: *Essential Evangelical Parallel Bible* by Oxford University Press

Reading Bibles:

- *THE MESSAGE (MSG)* (Eugene Peterson)
- *The New Living Translation (NLT)*
- *The New Testament in Modern English (PHILLIPS)* (J.B. Phillips)

Theology:

*Systematic Theology* by Wayne Grudem

Reasoned Faith *(other books by the following authors are also highly recommended)*:

*Mere Christianity* by C.S. Lewis

*A Reason for God* by Timothy Keller

The Christian Life *(other books by the following authors are also highly recommended)*:

Grief and loss: *A Grace Disguised* by Jerry L. Sittser

Peace and acceptance: *Be Still My Soul* by Elisabeth Elliot

Spiritual warfare:

- *The Screwtape Letters* by C.S. Lewis
- *Spiritual Warfare: How to Stand Firm in the Faith* by Ray C. Stedman

# • Day 1 •

*Pray.*

*Practice:* Job 23:10—*"He knows the way that I take; when He has tested me, I will come forth as gold."*

*Read:* Pages 7–9 (Publisher's Preface)

*Examine and Respond:*

1. In the preface of *Let God Be God*, we read two lists of questions and mysteries that the book of Job will address. Which of these questions resonate most with you?

2. Where in Scripture do we see that God welcomes our questions? Examine the verses below.

   a. Proverbs 3:13—

   b. Jeremiah 33:3—

   c. Matthew 7:7—

   d. James 1:5—

   e. Recall what you have read in the gospels. How did Jesus respond when people asked Him questions?

3. On page 9 of *Let God Be God*, we are told that the story of Job will instruct, inspire, and comfort us. How does this relate to what we read about Scripture in 2 Timothy 3:16–17?

4. Read Romans 8:18–39. List several truths from this passage that would have helped Job in his suffering and can still help us now. Take time to thank the Lord that no question of ours and no suffering on our paths will ever separate us from the love of Jesus Christ our Lord.

# • Day 2 •

*Pray.*

*Practice:*  Job 23:10—*"He knows the way that I take; when He has tested me, I will come forth as gold."*

*Read:*  Pages 11–13 (Chapter 1 Introduction and "An Epic Drama, A Record of History")

*Examine and Respond:*

1.  On page 12, Stedman notes that the question of why we suffer is the toughest question of our existence. Do you agree? If not, is there a different question that comes to mind?

2.  According to Stedman, questions that *"throb at the heart of the book of Job"* (page 12) include: *"Doesn't He care? Has he forgotten us? Has He turned His back on us?"* Do these remind you of Jesus' cries as He suffered? What did Jesus plead when facing suffering, and what can we learn from His response?

| Verse | What Jesus Did or Said | What We Learn from Jesus' Example |
|---|---|---|
| Matthew 26:39 | | |
| Matthew 26:42 | | |
| Matthew 26:44 | | |
| Matthew 27:46 | | |

3.  How does it sit with you that Job *"questions God, seeks answers from God, and even becomes angry with God—yet remains faithful"* (page 13)? How can someone question God and get angry at God, and yet remain faithful? Explain.

4.  Read 2 Timothy 2:13 and write it below in your own words. Thank God for His faithfulness that does not depend on ours!

# • Day 3 •

*Pray.*

*Practice:*  Job 23:10— *"He knows the way that I take; when He has tested me, I will come forth as gold."*

*Read:*  Pages 13–14 ("The Battleground")

*Examine and Respond:*

1.  How regularly do you think of battles in the spiritual realm when you endure or observe suffering? How might it help you to think of this more?

2.  How does Ephesians 6:10–13 apply to what you read in this section of *Let God Be God?*

3.  *"Human beings only love You out of self-interest..."* accuses Satan (page 14). Have you noticed this phenomenon in your own life? Are you prone to thinking more favorably of God when things go well than when life feels hard?

4.  How do the following Scriptures shed light on this issue? What do they tell us about God?

    a. Malachi 3:6—

    b. Hebrews 13:8—

    c. James 1:17—

5.  Take time to thank the Lord for His changelessness. He is our Rock and our Firm Foundation. In the storms of life, He will never change.

# • Day 4 •

*Pray.*

*Practice:*    Job 23:10—*"He knows the way that I take; when He has tested me, I will come forth as gold."*

*Read:*    Pages 14–16 ("An Overview of Job")

*Examine and Respond:*

1.    *"Though reeling from his losses, Job responds in faith"* (page 15). In your own words, write what Job says in Job 1:21.

2.    In Job 2:10, Job asks his wife the rhetorical question, *"Shall we accept good from God, and not trouble?"* How does this question help reframe life's hardships?

3.    *"In all this, Job did not sin in what he said"* (Job 2:10). What do we read in the book of James about how hard it is *not* to sin with our words? Read James 3:2–8 and summarize it here.

4.    Job's friends' argument *"sounds logical, unless you are the one who is suffering"* (page 16). David, a man after God's own heart, certainly laments about the prosperity of the wicked. What does David say, for example, in Psalm 73:3?

5.    How would a *shift of expectation* help us—i.e., coming to terms with the fact that many who live without God seem to do great, and those who follow Jesus seem to endure much suffering? How does seeing life from an eternal perspective help us, too, as we realize that these limited years on earth are not all there is?

# • Day 5 •

*Pray.*

*Practice:*   Job 23:10—*"He knows the way that I take; when He has tested me, I will come forth as gold."*

*Read:*       Pages 16–19 ("The Answer of the Lord")

*Examine and Respond:*

1. It is good to stop and consider how profound it is that *God answers.* What does this fact show us about the character of God?

2. How does this thought from page 17 sit with you? *"Ultimately, we must accept the fact that God does not exist for man, but man exists for God. We are God's instruments, and we exist to carry out His plans and purposes, which transcend our limited understanding."* Do you agree? Does this bother you, or console you, or … ? Relate this idea to what you read in Ephesians 2:10.

3. Why did God not double the number of Job's offspring the way He had doubled the size of Job's herds? (What was true about Job's first ten children? Stedman discusses this on page 17.) How can this idea help us as we process the deaths of our loved ones who trusted in the Lord?

4. *"God never explains to Job why he has suffered so intensely"* (page 18). What role do faith and trust play in our ability to suffer well? How does this relate to 1 Corinthians 13:12?

5. *"God never lets go of Job, and Job never lets go of God"* (page 18). Insert your own name into that sentence instead of Job's, and record it here:

   Read the second part of Hebrews 13:5 and paraphrase it here:

   It has been thousands of years, but God hasn't forsaken His people yet—and He never will. *"And surely I am with you always, to the very end of the age"* (Matthew 28:20).

# • Day 6 •

*Pray.*

*Practice:*  Job 23:10— *"He knows the way that I take; when He has tested me, I will come forth as gold."*

*Read:*  Page 23 (Chapter 2 Introduction)

*Examine and Respond:*

1.  One version of the Nicene Creed is reprinted below. Read it aloud, keeping in mind what you now know about the lives of its writers:

    *We believe in one God, the Father, the Almighty, maker of heaven and earth, of all that is, seen and unseen.*

    *We believe in one Lord, Jesus Christ, the only Son of God, eternally begotten of the Father, God from God, Light from Light, true God from true God, begotten, not made, of one Being with the Father; through Him all things were made. For us and for our salvation He came down from heaven; by the power of the Holy Spirit He became incarnate from the Virgin Mary, and was made man. For our sake He was crucified under Pontius Pilate; He suffered death and was buried. On the third day He rose again in accordance with the Scriptures; He ascended into heaven and is seated at the right hand of the Father. He will come again in glory to judge the living and the dead, and His kingdom will have no end.*

    *We believe in the Holy Spirit, the Lord, the giver of life, who proceeds from the Father and the Son, who with the Father and the Son is worshiped and glorified, who has spoken through the Prophets. We believe in one holy catholic\* and apostolic\*\* Church. We acknowledge one baptism for the forgiveness of sins. We look for the resurrection of the dead, and the life of the world to come. Amen.*

    *\* universal    \*\* rooted in the historic teaching of the apostles*

2.  Do you feel *"entitled to a life of ease, comfort, and prosperity"* (page 23)? If so, why do you think this is? If not, what has happened in your life to cause you to shift away from this mindset?

3.  Summarize the following verses, with added notes about how they apply to you:

    a. 1 Peter 2:21—                              b. 1 Peter 4:12–13—

# • Day 7 •
Job 1:1–5

*Pray.*

*Practice:*   Job 23:10—*"He knows the way that I take; when He has tested me, I will come forth as gold."*

*Read:*   Pages 23–26 ("A Blameless and Upright Man")

*Examine and Respond:*

1.  In the first verse of Job, what four aspects of Job's character are listed? Are these the four adjectives you would most value being said about you? How do you want to be known?

2.  The words *"blameless"* and *"upright"* are used to refer to at least two others in the Bible.

    a. How is Noah described in Genesis 6:9?

    b. What does God command of Abraham in Genesis 17:1?

    c. We know that these men were not perfect, so what do *"blameless"* and *"upright"* mean?

    d. Would you be able to consider yourself *"blameless"* and *"upright"* in the Biblical sense?

3.  In Job 1:1, we see the phrase *"he feared God and shunned evil."* We also read similar phrases in Proverbs as characteristics of one who is wise. Paraphrase the following verses:

    a. Proverbs 3:7—                                   b. Proverbs 14:16—

4.  Why do you think the author of the book of Job writes a description of Job's character before we are told anything else about him?

5.  In Job 1:3, we see the prosperity of Job, and that he wasn't merely rich; he was actually *famous* for his wealth. How do you reconcile sacrificial Christian living and material wealth?

6.  What inspires you about Job's example as a father? Where did his priorities appear to lie? What habits did he put in place? How can you learn from his example and apply this?

# • Day 8 •
Job 1:6–12

*Pray.*

*Practice:*   Job 23:10— *"He knows the way that I take; when He has tested me, I will come forth as gold."*

*Read:*      Pages 26–28 ("From the Physical to the Invisible")

*Examine and Respond:*

1. Look up Ephesians 1:3 in two different Bible versions. Write the verse in your preferred version in the space below, taking a moment to pray it aloud.

2. When you hear the phrase *"the heavenly realms,"* what image or description comes to mind?

3. Read 2 Kings 6:15–17 and Acts 7:54–60 and record a brief summary of each story below.

4. Where is the *"heavenly realm"* we read about in the above verses? Stedman elaborates on this on page 26.

5. Who are these *"sons of God"* in Job 1:6? Read about them in Job 15:8, Psalm 29:1, and Isaiah 6:1–8 for insight.

6. C.S. Lewis, in *The Screwtape Letters*, describes one of Satan's major ploys as getting humans to downplay his existence and activity. What do we read in 1 Peter 5:8?

7. One rule-of-thumb of Bible interpretation is *Scriptura sacra sui ipsius interpres,* or *"sacred Scripture is its own interpreter."* Scriptures are best interpreted in light of other Scriptures, and the Bible must be considered as a whole. With this in mind, consider the following question: While Satan surely is living and active, as we read in 1 Peter 5:8 and see played out in Job, what perspective and hope do we gain from the truth expressed in 1 John 4:4? Should we be *afraid* of Satan?

# • Day 9 •

Job 1:6–12

*Pray.*

*Practice:*   Job 23:10—*"He knows the way that I take; when He has tested me, I will come forth as gold."*

*Read:*   Pages 28–30 ("A Strange War")

*Examine and Respond:*

1. Satan asks permission, and Satan answers God. This is a crucial hierarchy to remember! How can remembering this help you when you face temptation, testing, or trials?

2. In *Systematic Theology*, Wayne Grudem describes *sovereignty* as follows: *"God's sovereignty is His exercise of rule (as "sovereign" or "king") over His creation."* What do we learn in Job 1:6–12 about the sovereignty of God?

3. *"What we are witnessing here is not a battle in the conventional sense. It is not warfare—and certainly not war between two equal forces. God clearly has authority over Satan. If this is not warfare, what is it? It's a test"* (page 29). What difference does it make to you that what we read in Job is a *test*? What difference would it make to you in a time of your own suffering if you knew that what you were going through were actually a *test*? What difference in mindset would that provide?

4. Can you think of another instance in Scripture where we see Satan testing someone holy? See Luke 4.

5. How did Jesus respond to being tested? What did He use to stand firm?

6. Why might God allow tests? What do they accomplish? Think back to a test you have faced and reflect on any good that it produced.

# • Day 10 •
Job 1:6–12

*Pray.*

*Practice:* Job 23:10—*"He knows the way that I take; when He has tested me, I will come forth as gold."*

*Read:* Pages 30–31 ("The Satanic Activity and the Satanic Philosophy")

*Examine and Respond:*

1. In 1 Peter 5:8, we read advice about how to respond to Satan's prowling activity: *"Be sober minded; be watchful."* What does being *"sober-minded"* and *"watchful"* actually look like in our day-to-day lives?

2. In Ephesians 4:26–27, we are told how not to give Satan a foothold in our lives. Put Paul's advice in your own words here, along with any tangible, practical tips toward that effort.

3. On page 30, Stedman notes that Satan's philosophy could be described as *"Me first."*

   a. How do you see *"Me first"* played out in our modern culture, or in your own life?

   b. How does Satan's *"Me first"* philosophy contrast with that of Christ and what is to be expected of Christ's followers? See Philippians 2:5–8 and Matthew 16:24.

4. Examine Job 1:9–10.

   a. What two questions does Satan ask God in these verses?

   b. It is not a new strategy for Satan to introduce questions of doubt. What four words did he use to preface the question he asked of Eve in Genesis 3:1?

   c. Does Satan work the same way in your life at times? In what area(s) are you prone to doubt? What practical "weapons for battle" can you employ to fight off those thoughts?

# • Day 11 •
Job 1:13–19

*Pray.*

*Practice:* 1 John 4:4 (ESV)—*"He who is in you is greater than he who is in the world."*

*Read:* Pages 31–33 ("The Rules of the Test")

*Examine and Respond:*

1. On page 31 of Stedman's commentary, we read that boundaries can ultimately provide us freedom. What do *we* gain from God's setting boundaries to Satan's activities? How does it help you to know that Satan is limited by God?

2. In Job 1:13–18, we see loss after loss come to Job. List his losses in the table below.

| Naturalistic Causes | Supernatural Causes |
|---|---|
| | |

3. We benefit from hindsight and written history to know that Satan is working behind the scenes in Job's sufferings, but what *might* Job have concluded about the cause of his losses?

4. What do the following verses tell us about why suffering sometimes occurs in our lives?

   a. Psalm 38:3–5—                         b. Romans 5:3–5—

5. Why did neither of the above Scriptural instances for suffering apply to Job?

6. Do you find yourself wondering *"WHY?!"* when you go through hard times? Are you prone to blaming Satan, attributing your suffering to your own sin, resigning yourself to not knowing the "why"s, or ... ? Does it help us to know "why" when we are going through hard times? Why might God not always let us know "why"? Explain.

# • Day 12 •
Job 1:13–19

*Pray.*

*Practice:* 1 John 4:4 (ESV)—*"He who is in you is greater than he who is in the world."*

*Read:* Pages 33–34 ("Defending God")

*Examine and Respond:*

1. Piles of books are written about *theodicy*—reconciling the existence of an all-good, all-powerful God with the existence of evil (page 33). Anchoring ourselves in the truth of God's goodness and power, no matter what is happening around us, in us, or to us, is essential—and God's people have needed to do this since the dawn of human history.

   a. What two truths about God does King David pen in Psalm 62:11–12?

   b. What would it be like if God were only strong, but not loving?

   c. What would it be like if God were only loving, but not strong?

   d. What does it mean to you, in a current trial, to know that God is both strong *and* loving?

2. Read Psalm 103 aloud. Here, David describes the same God who allowed Job to endure extreme and total suffering. Clearly, there exist both depth and mystery in the ways of God.

3. Read how Eugene Peterson translates what God says in Isaiah 55:8 (MSG):

   *"I don't think the way you think.*
   *The way you work isn't the way I work..."*

   How can this truth actually be a comfort to us rather than a frustration?

4. Write Romans 11:33–36 in your own words, making it your prayer.

# • Day 13 •
Job 1:20–22

*Pray.*

*Practice:*    1 John 4:4 (ESV)—*"He who is in you is greater than he who is in the world."*

*Read:*    Pages 34–36 ("Job Responds to His Pain and Loss")

*Examine and Respond:*

1. How would *you* respond to the incredible loss that Job has just suffered, if it had happened to you?

2. How does Job express his grief in Job 1:20?

3. How does Job express his devotion to God in Job 1:20–22?

4. Does Job take credit here for any of what he originally had? Explain the idea of "grace vs. merit" and how it applies here.

5. How does Job's worship prove that Satan's claim in Job 1:9 was false?

6. How does Job's worship guide our own in instances when God allows a terrible loss?

7. Write a prayer of worship and commitment, determining to bring God your *"sacrifice of praise"* (Hebrews 13:15) even—or especially!—when life's next hard trial comes your way.

*Pray.*

*Practice:*   1 John 4:4 (ESV)—*"He who is in you is greater than he who is in the world."*

*Read:*   Pages 37–38 (Chapter 3 Introduction)

*Examine and Respond:*

1.  We read in this section of *Let God Be God* the story of Dr. Paul Brand, who once found himself grateful for the sensation of pain. Can you relate? Have you ever felt grateful for pain?

2.  By definition, *pain hurts.* It came as a result of the Fall and will have no place in heaven—yet God is too good and loves us too much to waste our pain when we encounter it on earth. He infuses our pain with purpose and is present every moment of our suffering. How does Psalm 23 affirm that God is present even in the midst of severe and painful trials?

3.  In Job 2:2, what do we see again here in terms of sovereignty and accountability? Who is accountable to whom?

4.  In Job 2:3, what are we to make of the Lord's statement that Satan *"incited"* Him against Job *"without reason"*? The Lord is acknowledging that the test was needless and that Job did not deserve this treatment; but this can also strike us as troubling, since it might appear from this verse that God is admitting that He was tricked or manipulated. What is your take? What does God mean when he says that Satan *"incited"* him against Job *"to destroy him without reason"*?

5.  Write out Revelation 21:4 below. How can our certain hope of someday having *no more pain* help you persevere and gain perspective through the pains of this life?

# • Day 15 •
Job 2:1–3

*Pray.*

*Practice:*     1 John 4:4 (ESV)—*"He who is in you is greater than he who is in the world."*

*Read:*         Pages 38–39 ("Perspective Makes All the Difference")

*Examine and Respond:*

1. Although we cannot see behind the scenes of our lives during times of pressure and trials, we do know that God is there, He is for us, He will accomplish His good purposes, Satan will never defeat us, and our affliction is never meaningless. Due to our lives' placements in Biblical history, what advantages over Job do we have?

2. The gift of Scripture is not to be underestimated. It gives us the peek *"behind the curtain"* that Job did not have. How can having the following Scriptures help us during our trials? Of what do they assure us?

   a. Isaiah 43:2—

   b. Romans 8:18–39—

   c. 1 Corinthians 10:13—

   d. 2 Corinthians 4:17—

   e. James 1:12—

   f. 1 Peter 5:10—

   *And more!*

# • Day 16 •
### Job 2:4–6

*Pray.*

*Practice:*    1 John 4:4 (ESV)—*"He who is in you is greater than he who is in the world."*

*Read:*    Pages 39–41 (" 'Skin for Skin!' ")

*Examine and Respond:*

1.  The same Satan who tormented Job, with God's permission, is still at work today. What are practical steps you can take to prepare for what we see Satan about to do to Job? That is, what can you do *now* to ready yourself for the times in life when you are troubled in your flesh (health) and bones (thoughts/emotions/subconscious)?

2.  Although Satan is still at work, God is also still at work! The good news, as Stedman reminds us on page 40, is that *"there is a divine limitation to the power of Satan."* Examine other limits of Satan by looking up Scriptures in the chart below. These are just some of the many limits that bind our adversary.

|  | *God* | *Satan* | *Notes* |
|---|---|---|---|
| *Location* | God is omnipresent: Psalm 121:3 and Proverbs 15:3. | Satan cannot be everywhere at the same time; he must travel around: 1 Peter 5:8 and Job 1:7. | |
| *Power* | God is omnipotent; He is all-powerful and reigns supreme: Revelation 19:1, 6 and Luke 1:37. | Satan is not in full control; His power is limited by God: 1 John 5:18. | |
| *Knowledge* | God is omniscient; He sees all and knows all: Psalm 147:5 and Psalm 139:2. | Satan does not know everything; notice in Matthew 4:1–11 that Satan does not know ahead of time how Jesus will respond. | |
| *Creation* | God alone is the Creator: Isaiah 45:18 and Psalm 103:20. | Satan is a created being and is not equal to God: Isaiah 14:11–13. | |
| *Destiny* | No matter what we face in this life, *Christ won*: 2 Corinthians 15:57, Romans 8:37–39, and the *Resurrection!* | Satan's destiny is already determined; he will lose the final battle: Revelation 20:10. | |

# • Day 17 •
Job 2:4–6

*Pray.*

*Practice:* 1 John 4:4 (ESV)—*"He who is in you is greater than he who is in the world."*

*Read:* Pages 41–43 ("Does God Know What He's Doing?")

*Examine and Respond:*

1.  a. How would you summarize Isaiah 40:25–31 in your own words?

    b. What does this passage of Isaiah have to do with Job 2:4–6 and what you read in this section of *Let God Be God*?

2.  Read Jeremiah 18:1–6 and Isaiah 64:8.

    a. What does the metaphor in these verses have to do with Job?

    b. How does this metaphor relate to us?

3.  How does a potter work his clay? What does he do to the clay? What steps does it take for the clay to become a finished product? How does this apply to us, as clay in our Potter's hands?

4.  What do we read about God in Psalm 103:8–17 that can help us trust Him fully as clay in His loving hands?

# • Day 18 •
Job 2:7–9

*Pray.*

*Practice:*   1 John 4:4 (ESV)—*"He who is in you is greater than he who is in the world."*

*Read:*   Pages 43–45 ("The Attack of Job's Wife")

*Examine and Respond:*

1. Here we see Satan's first attack on Job's body. Whatever illness this was, *"it turned him into a pitiful, repulsive, horrifying figure"* (page 43). Can you relate to this in any way?

2. In what way is Job's wife echoing the plea of Satan?

3. What motive did Satan have for wanting Job to curse God? Is this the same motive as Job's wife's?

4. What practical application can we make from seeing this negative example of Job's wife? The Bible is full of guidelines for our speech, and how we speak to our spouses is no exception! Note what each of these verses tells us about how we should speak:

   a. Proverbs 15:1—                          b. Proverbs 31:26—

   c. James 1:19—                             d. Ephesians 4:29—

   e. Colossians 4:6—

5. When do you find yourself most prone to speak unhelpful words? Take some time to identify this, then notice it next time, and pray for strength to speak words that represent Christ and strengthen the hearer. We need—*and have access to!*—God's help in this; it is not simply a determined self-improvement project. The Holy Spirit will equip us for every good work. Psalm 19:14 is a helpful daily—even moment-by-moment—prayer. In the space below, write this verse in your own words, making it your prayer.

# • Day 19 •
Job 2:10

*Pray.*

*Practice:*    1 John 4:4 (ESV)—*"He who is in you is greater than he who is in the world."*

*Read:*      Pages 45–46 ("Job's Gentle Rebuke")

*Examine and Respond:*

1. Job's response to his wife is threefold and gives us much from which to learn:

   a. What example does Job set for us when we see him telling his wife that she is *"talking foolishly"* rather than simply calling her a fool?

   b. What do we learn from Job when he asks his wife, *"Shall we accept good from God, and not trouble?"*? What does this show us about Job's view of God and his expectations for life?

   c. What can we learn from the fact that *"In all this, Job did not sin in what he said"*? (You may remember this verse from Day 4; it is an idea worth revisiting.)

2. While Job seems to hold the opinion that life has both good and trouble, and we must accept both, Job's wife seems to maintain the philosophy that *"life ought always to be pleasant."*

   a. Do you think this philosophy of Job's wife has always been rampant, or do you think it is stronger in some cultures or times more than others?

   b. Is *"life ought always to be pleasant"* a dominating philosophy in our culture today? How do you see it manifested?

   c. Do you ever find yourself maintaining this *"life ought always to be pleasant"* philosophy?

   d. What are practical ways to battle this worldview in your own heart and mind? Take time to pray for God's help in this.

# • Day 20 •
Job 2:11–13

*Pray.*

*Practice:* 1 John 4:4 (ESV)—*"He who is in you is greater than he who is in the world."*

*Read:* Pages 46–48 ("The Most Devastating Assault")

*Examine and Respond:*

1.  What are the motives of Job's friends when they decide to visit Job?

2.  What does it mean that Job's friends essentially held a funeral service for him, performing ancient rites that were reserved for the dead? How do you think Job may have felt about this?

3.  Pretend that you do not know what will happen in the next chapter. What would you expect Job's friends to say to him in the following chapters, given their intentions? What would *you* have said to Job if you were one of his friends?

4.  On page 48 in *Let God Be God*, Stedman rephrases several key Biblical truths that bring great perspective and comfort. Although Scripture abounds with evidence for these truths, just one verse per point is listed below. Look up each verse and make a note beside it.

| Stedman, page 48 | Scripture |
|---|---|
| *"God Himself allows trials in our lives. They come to us by His permission."* | Lamentations 3:37–38— |
| *"God is at work, even in your suffering."* | Romans 8:28— |
| *"He does not delight in our suffering."* | Lamentations 3:31–33— |
| *"God guards and keeps us."* | 2 Thessalonians 3:3— |
| *"God teaches us that we are stronger in Him than we ever imagined."* | Philippians 4:13— |
| *"His life and power are strong in us."* | Ephesians 1:18–19— |

# • Day 21 •
Job 3:1–10

*Pray.*

*Practice:* Psalm 91:1–2—*"Whoever dwells in the shelter of the Most High will rest in the shadow of the Almighty. I will say of the LORD, 'He is my refuge and my fortress, my God, in whom I trust.' "*

*Read:* Pages 49–51 (Chapter 4 Introduction and "Job's Only Alternative")

*Examine and Respond:*

1. Stedman states on page 50 that *"God is good. His love endures forever. If He allows pain or problems to come into our lives, He does so for reasons that are good, perfect, and loving. We need to learn that our only righteous response is one of blessing God and acknowledging His goodness."* However, we also read in Scripture that Jesus *wept*; we do not see Him singing praises at the bedside of dead Lazarus. Is it possible to grieve while simultaneously blessing God and acknowledging His goodness? What does this look like?

2. In Job 3:1–10, Job alternates between the themes of day and night. When Job curses the day he was born, we see echoes of Genesis 1. For example, when Job declares in Job 3:4, *"Let that day be darkness!"*, we see a reversal of what God declared in Genesis 1:3, *"Let there be light."*

   a. The theme of darkness and light is used to refer to both death and life, as well as to what is hidden and what is revealed. How does each of these apply to the sufferings of Job?

      • Death and life:

      • What is hidden and what is revealed:

   b. How can you relate to Job in this passage, where he curses the day of his birth and implies that what should have been a bright beginning of life feels like the darkness of death? Have you ever felt things that you know are the opposite of how God intended them to be? Explain.

3. In Job 3:5, the verb translated *"claim"* is the same word used for God's wonderful acts of salvation on Israel's behalf elsewhere in the Old Testament; it is often translated *"redeem."* (For example, see Exodus 6:6 and Isaiah 43:1.) Why would Job use such a theologically loaded word? What does this show us about Job? How does it show the depth of his despair? What does it demonstrate about his knowledge of God?

4. Stedman states on page 51 that *"If we could see some reason for what we have to go through, we could more easily endure it. But pointless trouble is corrosive to our souls."* Do you agree? What do we know from Scripture, and what do we know of God, that assures us our troubles are *never* pointless?

# • Day 22 •
## Job 3:11–26

*Pray.*

*Practice:* Psalm 91:1–2—*"Whoever dwells in the shelter of the Most High will rest in the shadow of the Almighty. I will say of the LORD, 'He is my refuge and my fortress, my God, in whom I trust.' "*

*Read:* Pages 52–53 ("A Primitive View of Death")

*Examine and Respond:*

1. In this section, Job describes the afterlife as a time of rest: *"solitude and quiet after the tumult and trouble of life."* Stedman notes that at this point in the story, Job has a much more primitive view of death than we read of in the New Testament. Why is it important to have an accurate view of what happens after we die? How does our view of the afterlife affect our life here and now?

2. In Job 3:23, Job says that he has been *"hedged in"* by God. He seems to mean this in a negative sense, as something oppressive. Supporting this idea is the fact that he also refers to God as a taskmaster in Job 3:18. But this rare Hebrew word for *"hedged in"* is also used in Job 1:10, where Satan says that God has *"put a hedge"* of protective blessing around Job. The verb is rare enough that the echo is probably not coincidental.

   a. What does the fact that Job appears to view God's hedging him in as negative, rather than as a blessing, imply about how Job may be misunderstanding his position before God?

   b. Are you prone to viewing God's boundaries for your life—His *"hedging you in"*—as negative rather than positive? How so? In what areas?

   c. When in your life did you feel as though God were restricting you from something, and you realized only later that He was actually protecting you?

   d. Read Psalm 91 and take time to thank the Lord for His ceaseless presence and protection. Our souls are off-limits to Satan, and our eternal destiny is secure.

# • Day 23 •
Job 4:1–11

*Pray.*

*Practice:*   Psalm 91:1–2—*"Whoever dwells in the shelter of the Most High will rest in the shadow of the Almighty. I will say of the LORD, 'He is my refuge and my fortress, my God, in whom I trust.' "*

*Read:*   Pages 54–56 ("Job's Friends Respond")

*Examine and Respond:*

1.   Record what you know of Job's three friends so far (described by Stedman on page 54).

| Friend | Stedman's Nickname | Characteristics |
|--------|-------------------|-----------------|
| Eliphaz | | |
| Bildad | | |
| Zophar | | |

2.   While Job's three friends each have their own points to make, they all seem to believe deeply that whatever people receive in life is a direct result of their behavior. How would you summarize Eliphaz's main points in 4:1–11?

3.   How do the life, suffering, and death of Jesus directly contradict what Eliphaz is implying (that the righteous are never punished and that only the unrighteous suffer)?

4.   Eliphaz asks Job a rhetorical question in Job 4:6: *"Should not your piety be your confidence and your blameless ways your hope?"* This sounds fine—perhaps even kind and encouraging—but we know better than this. In what (or in whom) should we actually be placing our confidence and hope? (Certainly not in any good works!)

5.   Write out Psalm 71:5 in the space below, making it your prayer.

# • Day 24 •
Job 4:12–21

*Pray.*

*Practice:*   Psalm 91:1–2—*"Whoever dwells in the shelter of the Most High will rest in the shadow of the Almighty. I will say of the LORD, 'He is my refuge and my fortress, my God, in whom I trust.'"*

*Read:*   Pages 56–59 ("A Disturbing Passage")

*Examine and Respond:*

1.  Eliphaz tells Job about a supernatural experience he has had. Of course, the Lord still works in supernatural ways and gives people words to speak to others. Of course, too, sometimes a person claims to have *"a word from the Lord"* that is not actually of God. So how do we know if someone's *"word from the Lord"* is really from the Lord?

2.  On pages 57 and 58, how does Stedman explain what is true of *true* angels sent from the *true* God?

3.  Although we read nuggets of truth in Eliphaz's speech to Job, Eliphaz seems to view God only as a God of justice. He sees nothing of the love, compassion, forgiveness, and patience of God. Because of his unbalanced and incomplete theology, even the limited truth that Eliphaz speaks becomes a lie.

    a. How can we guard against such theological imbalance in our own lives?

    b. Why is it vital to know the truth about who God is? How does that knowledge affect us in our day-to-day living?

4.  There are many Bible verses that combat the eloquent arguments of Eliphaz. Note what Luke 12:7 says is true of God and His concern for us.

# • Day 25 •
Job 5

*Pray.*

*Practice:*    Psalm 91:1–2—*"Whoever dwells in the shelter of the Most High will rest in the shadow of the Almighty. I will say of the LORD, 'He is my refuge and my fortress, my God, in whom I trust.' "*

*Read:*    Pages 59–62 ("Sly Accusations" and "The Flawed Theology of Eliphaz")

*Examine and Respond:*

1. Eliphaz's speech continues in Job 5. Put on your "critic's hat" and practice sorting out truth from falsehood. Pick one true statement that Eliphaz says to Job in this chapter, and one that is either misleading or completely false.

   a. True:



   b. Misleading/False:




2. How does reading Eliphaz's speech reinforce to you the benefit of studying Bible verses both in their specific contexts and in light of the Bible in its entirety?




3. How can the principles in the verses below apply to what we read from Eliphaz?

   a. 1 John 4:1—                          b. 1 Thessalonians 5:20–22—




4. God's truth holds up against skepticism. Questioning is *good* when we are comparing what we hear to the truth of what we know of God's character and His Word. What can we learn from the example of the Bereans? See Acts 17:11.

# • Day 26 •
Job 6

*Pray.*

*Practice:*    Psalm 91:1–2—*"Whoever dwells in the shelter of the Most High will rest in the shadow of the Almighty. I will say of the LORD, 'He is my refuge and my fortress, my God, in whom I trust.' "*

*Read:*    Pages 62–65 ("Job's Reply to Eliphaz")

*Examine and Respond:*

    1.   a. Restate Job 6:14 in your own words.


          b. How is it possible, with the best of intentions, to fail to show kindness to someone who is desperately hurting? Do you have any experience with this?


    2.   Job essentially says that his complaining helps him to cope with his troubles. How can you relate to this? Give an example.


    3.   What does the Bible have to say about complaining? Explore this in the verses below.

          a. What was God's response to the Israelites' grumbling? See Numbers 11:1 as an example.


          b. What does Philippians 2:14 tell us about complaining?


          c. If we are not supposed to complain, how do we carry out verses like Galatians 6:2, which says to *"Bear one another's burdens"*? How can we bear burdens that we do not know about? How can we help people through their hardship if we do not know that things are hard for them? What is the balance here? How do we share things that are hard for us with a godly approach instead of in a grumbling way? Record your thoughts below.

# • Day 27 •
## Job 7

*Pray.*

*Practice:*  Psalm 91:1–2—*"Whoever dwells in the shelter of the Most High will rest in the shadow of the Almighty. I will say of the LORD, 'He is my refuge and my fortress, my God, in whom I trust.' "*

*Read:*  Pages 65–68 ("Job Addresses God")

*Examine and Respond:*

1.  We saw in Job 6 how Job responds to his friends; now, in Job 7, he addresses God. How does the thought expressed by the psalmist in Psalm 8:4 echo Job's words in 7:17–18?

    a. Record Psalm 8:4 in the space below.

    b. Comparing Psalm 8:4 with Job 7:17–18, we are reminded of how the same fact can be completely transformed by perspective. What is the same about the facts expressed in these verses, and what seems different about the perspective or tone?

    • Similar fact expressed:

    • Different perspective or tone:

2.  We know that God has emotion—so what do you imagine God would be feeling as He hears Job in Job 7?

3.  Stedman makes many important points on pages 67–68. Write down something that sticks out to you that you would like to tuck away and remember.

4.  In times of suffering, what insight and encouragement can you gain from Ephesians 3:12–13?

# • Day 28 •

*Pray.*

*Practice:*   Psalm 91:1–2—*"Whoever dwells in the shelter of the Most High will rest in the shadow of the Almighty. I will say of the LORD, 'He is my refuge and my fortress, my God, in whom I trust.' "*

*Read:*        Pages 69–70 (Chapter 5 Introduction)

*Examine and Respond:*

1.  How has your perspective of human suffering changed over the course of your life?

2.  Stedman states on page 70, *"It's easy to be 'Job's comforter.' It's easy to offer simplistic answers to our suffering friends. But it takes courage and honesty to admit that there are no easy answers to the problem of pain."* How does the mystery of suffering, or its lack of easy answers, sit with you?

3.  The following verses all convey the same anchoring truth, which is what?

    a. Psalm 100:3—                                    b. Isaiah 43:1—

    c. 1 Corinthians 6:19–20—                    d. Galatians 3:29—

4.  How does the truth in the above verses—that *we are not our own but we belong to Christ*—shed light on the mystery of suffering? Said another way: Knowing that we belong fully to Christ assures us of what in terms of our suffering?

5.  The Heidelberg Catechism (1563) asks as its first question, *"What is your only comfort in life and in death?"* The answer, shown below, elaborates on the reality of our belonging to Christ. Read it aloud to close today's study:

    My only comfort in life and in death is *"That I am not my own, but belong—body and soul, in life and in death—to my faithful Savior, Jesus Christ. He has fully paid for all my sins with His precious blood, and has set me free from the tyranny of the devil. He also watches over me in such a way that not a hair can fall from my head without the will of my Father in heaven; in fact, all things must work together for my salvation. Because I belong to Him, Christ, by His Holy Spirit, assures me of eternal life and makes me wholeheartedly willing and ready from now on to live for Him."*

# • Day 29 •
## Job 8

*Pray.*

*Practice:*  Psalm 91:1–2—*"Whoever dwells in the shelter of the Most High will rest in the shadow of the Almighty. I will say of the LORD, 'He is my refuge and my fortress, my God, in whom I trust.' "*

*Read:*  Pages 70–73 ("Bildad the Brutal")

*Examine and Respond:*

1.  Bildad seems to toe the party line and tries to get Job to admit his sin as the cause of his suffering. History disproves the veracity of this idea.

| Person Who Suffered | How He Suffered | Suffering a Direct Result of Sin? |
|---|---|---|
| Abel | | |
| Joseph | | |
| Jesus | | |
| Someone else in history: | | |
| An example in your life: | | |

2.  *"Bildad's style is to ask questions that focus on the logic of the argument. He is a cold, intellectual thinker and a hard-nosed debater"* (page 71). Can you relate? Is this like you, or like someone you know? Does intellectual, hard-nosed debate ever have a place in grief or human suffering?

3.  Put on your "critic's hat" again and weed through Bildad's speech. Pick one true statement that Bildad says to Job in Job 8 and one that is either misleading or completely false.

    a. True:

    b. Misleading/False:

4.  *"Bildad is speaking out of a wrong spirit..."* (page 73). May the Lord help us not to be Bildads. Merge Matthew 12:34 (*out of the abundance of our hearts, our mouths speak*) with Psalm 51:10 (*create in me a pure heart, O God...*) to write a prayer for God's help. We need it! He faithfully gives it.

# • Day 30 •

*Pray.*

*Practice:*   Psalm 91:1–2—*"Whoever dwells in the shelter of the Most High will rest in the shadow of the Almighty. I will say of the LORD, 'He is my refuge and my fortress, my God, in whom I trust.' "*

*Read:*   Pages 73–74 ("Three Flaws in the Thinking of Job's 'Comforters' ")

*Examine and Respond:*

The chart below lists three basic flaws in Job's friends' thinking. Fill in the rest of the chart, summarizing relevant Scriptures and noting how the situations may apply to you (what to do differently than Job's friends).

| Flaw | Relevant Scriptures | Application |
|---|---|---|
| Answering without first trying to find out the truth of Job's situation. | Proverbs 18:2—<br><br>Proverbs 18:13— | |
| Incomplete and narrow theology. | Jeremiah 9:23–24—<br><br>2 Peter 3:18—<br><br>1 John 4:6–7— | |
| Never asking God for help in understanding Job's problem or praying with him. | Psalm 121:1–2—<br><br>Matthew 18:20—<br><br>John 14:13–14—<br><br>James 1:5—<br><br>James 5:16—<br><br>1 John 5:14–15— | |

*Pray.*

*Practice:*    1 Thessalonians 5:11—*"Encourage one another and build each another up..."*

*Read:*    Pages 74–79 ("Who Can Judge the Judge?")

*Examine and Respond:*

1.  In Job 9:1–12, Job elaborates on the mighty powers of God. We who rest secure in God's love can take comfort in reflecting on the power of God. But someone who is not sure of his or her standing before God would feel differently about God's power, since as we explored on Day 12, absolute power without love is horrifying. Read Psalm 136 and note how David equally balances God's powerful works and God's great love for His people.

2.  Stedman explains that Job's words *"contain hints of the incarnation, the great underlying truth of the New Testament: the fact that God did truly limit Himself and become a man"* (page 78). Job does seem to long for a mediator, someone who will bridge the gap between Almighty God and frail man. How does Job express this desire in the following verses?

    a. Job 9:32–35—

    b. Job 10:4–5—

3.  Read Hebrews 4:14–16. How did Christ fulfill the longing of man, expressed by Job, for a mediator? *Thank the Lord for the gift of His Son.*

# • Day 32 •
Job 10:18–22

*Pray.*

*Practice:* 1 Thessalonians 5:11—*"Encourage one another and build each another up..."*

*Read:* Pages 79–81 ("Job's View of Death")

*Examine and Respond:*

1. When have you experienced the silence of God? How did it feel? How long did it last? Did you ever realize later why God may have chosen to be silent? Reflect on this experience.

2. What do we learn in the following verses about the perceived silence of God and its effect on the one crying out to Him?

   a. Psalm 28:1—                                      b. Psalm 109:1—

   c. Isaiah 64:12—                                     d. Habakkuk 1:13—

3. Most of the references to silence in Scripture are actually commands for *people* to be silent, written as a positive action, with "remaining silent" presented as something we are encouraged to do. Does knowing this help us "cut God some slack" when He seems silent?

4. We see in these verses of Job that Job does not seem to believe in an afterlife at this point in his spiritual journey. By observing Job on his journey, what hope can we gain for our own lives or the lives of loved ones whom we see camping out in areas of theological error? Must we have perfect theology for God to want to continue working in our lives? Does growth always happen quickly? Are "steps backward" ever a part of a Christian's journey? Should "steps backward" cause us to lose hope in God's working in our lives?

5. What encouragement can you find in the truth of Philippians 1:6? Record the verse below, writing it in the form of a prayer of confidence in God and what He promises to do in your life.

# • Day 33 •
Job 11

*Pray.*

*Practice:*   1 Thessalonians 5:11—*"Encourage one another and build each another up..."*

*Read:*      Pages 81–83 ("Zophar the Zealous")

*Examine and Respond:*

1.  Why do you think Zophar responds to Job in such a harsh way? The Bible does not tell us, but what are your ideas?

2.  Zophar is a prime negative example of how *not* to treat people when they are suffering, but the following Bible verses set up a helpful contrast. Summarize what each verse below says about how we should interact with others, especially those who are suffering.

    a. Romans 12:15—

    b. 1 Corinthians 12:26—

    c. Ephesians 4:1–2—

    d. 1 Thessalonians 5:11—

    e. 1 Thessalonians 5:14—

    f. 1 Peter 3:8—

3.  Stedman makes excellent points on page 83 that are worth re-reading. He explains the importance of extending beyond intellectual theology to the realm of true empathy.

    a. How does our *empathy* toward others depend on our *theology*? They are related!

    b. Is empathy something that you struggle with, or does it come easily to you?

    c. What are practical ways you can increase or demonstrate your empathy for others who are struggling?

# • Day 34 •
## Job 12

*Pray.*

*Practice:*   1 Thessalonians 5:11—*"Encourage one another and build each another up..."*

*Read:*   Pages 85–88 (Chapter 6 Introduction and "God Cannot Be Boxed In")

*Examine and Respond:*

1.   What is sarcastic about Job's response to his friends in the first few verses of Job 12?

2.   As you remember all that Job has endured, what is noteworthy about Job's pouring out praise to God in the last section of Job 12?

3.   Job acknowledges in Job 12:7–10 that even the beasts of the earth and all of nature affirm the power of God. This is a "given" throughout Scripture. Jot notes beside the example verses below.

   a. Psalm 19:1–6—

   b. Psalm 69:34—

   c. Psalm 96:11–12—

   d. Proverbs 3:19–20—

   e. Isaiah 43:20–21—

   f. Matthew 8:27—

   g. Luke 19:40—

   h. Romans 1:20—

   i. Circle the verse above that you appreciate most.

4.   In Job 12:7–9, Job points out distinct parts of creation that teach, tell, and declare to us that God is the one in control. What in nature points you best to God?

# • Day 35 •
Job 13:1–12

*Pray.*

*Practice:* 1 Thessalonians 5:11—*"Encourage one another and build each another up..."*

*Read:* Pages 88–90 ("The Wisest Thing You Can Say to a Hurting Person")

*Examine and Respond:*

1. In your own words, write the essence of what Job tells his friends in the following verses.

   a. Job 13:1–2—

   b. Job 13:3—

   c. Job 13:4— (What does it mean that they *"whitewash with lies"* and are *"worthless physicians"*?)

2. What does Job beg of his friends in this section? Specifically, note verses 5 and 13 of Job 13.

3. What does Job's request of his friends for silence have to do with what you answered on Day 32 (question 3)? How does understanding a human's need for silence shed insight on why God may sometimes choose to be silent?

4. When is a time you have wanted those around you simply to be silent? What were your reasons for this?

5. How do you know if/when your silence is the best gift to give a hurting friend?

6. Paraphrase the verses below.

   a. Proverbs 10:19—

   b. Proverbs 11:12—

   c. Ecclesiastes 3:7—

   d. How can you apply these verses to your life?

# • Day 36 •
Job 13:13–19

*Pray.*

*Practice:*   1 Thessalonians 5:11—*"Encourage one another and build each another up..."*

*Read:*   Pages 90–91 ("A Final Plea")

*Examine and Respond:*

1.  How does Stedman explain a potential misinterpretation of Job 13:15?

2.  Reading Job 13:15 in Bible translations that are "reading Bibles" rather than "study Bibles" (those that attempt to paraphrase by translating ideas and tone rather than individual words) confirms Stedman's point about Job 13:15. Read two such paraphrases below.

| New Living Translation | *"God might kill me, but I have no other hope. I am going to argue my case with Him."* |
|---|---|
| The Message | *"Because even if He killed me, I'd keep on hoping. I'd defend my innocence to the very end."* |

Even with alternate translations, Job seems to show admirable traits in this verse. Describe the good you see in his perspective.

3.  Job appears to feel confident to stand before God and defend himself.

    a. What does this show us about the character of Job and his relationship with God?

    b. How would *you* feel standing before God to "present your case" and defend yourself?

4.  We have the profound gift of Christ as our Defender and Intercessor. Read the following verses, paraphrase them, and turn them into prayers of gratitude to God. *"Thanks be to God for His indescribable gift!"* (2 Corinthians 9:15).

    a. Romans 8:34—                                      b. Hebrews 7:25—

    c. 1 John 2:1—

# • Day 37 •
Job 13:20–28

*Pray.*

*Practice:*   1 Thessalonians 5:11—*"Encourage one another and build each another up..."*

*Read:*   Pages 91–92 ("Job's Two-Part Request")

*Examine and Respond:*

1.  Job's first request of God in this passage (Job 13:20–21) is for God to lift the pain and anguish he is undergoing. Is that an acceptable request, or are we as Christians supposed to endure any suffering that comes our way, assuming it is the perfect will of God, without asking for relief? Examine the following Scriptures, making notes beside each reference.

    a. Psalm 6:1–4—

    b. Luke 22:42—

    c. 2 Corinthians 12:7–8—

    d. Having read the above verses, what can you conclude about the appropriateness of asking God to take away your suffering?

2.  Stedman explains on page 91: *"Though Job experiences doubt over what God is doing, though he feels misunderstood and mistreated, he respects the majesty of God."* This is key—but what exactly is the majesty of God? Examine the verses below.

    a. Exodus 15:6–7—               b. 1 Chronicles 29:11—

    c. Psalm 8:1—                    d. Psalm 93:1—

    e. Psalm 104:1—                  f. Psalm 145:5—

    g. After reading these verses, how would you describe *the majesty of God*?

    h. What good does it do a person to acknowledge and focus on God's majesty?

3.  In Job 13:22–23, Job sincerely asks God, *"What have I done? How have I offended You?"* David asks a similar question of God in Psalm 139:23–24. Why are these important questions? Look at Psalm 32:5, Psalm 51, and Proverbs 28:13 for some clues.

## • Day 38 •
Job 14:1–6

*Pray.*

*Practice:*  1 Thessalonians 5:11—*"Encourage one another and build each another up..."*

*Read:*  Bottom of page 92 through first half of page 93 ("Chapter One of the Great Story")

*Examine and Respond:*

1.  In the first five verses of Job 14, Job expresses the limits of human control. How does this idea contradict current popular thinking?

2.  Job explains in Job 14:5, *"Man's days are determined; You have decreed the number of his months..."* This is not an unfamiliar refrain in Scripture; a few examples are shown below. What do these verses say?

    a. Psalm 39:4–7—

    b. Psalm 78:38–39—

    c. James 4:14—

3.  What good does it do us to acknowledge the brevity of life?

4.  Read Psalm 90:12. Rewrite it as your own prayer below.

# • Day 39 •
Job 14:7–13

*Pray.*

*Practice:*　1 Thessalonians 5:11—*"Encourage one another and build each another up..."*

*Read:*　Second half of pg. 93 through first half of pg. 95 ("Chapter One of the Great Story," cont.)

*Examine and Respond:*

1.　Stedman writes on page 94: *"In his pain, Job has come to a pessimistic view of life. Though there is much truth in what he says, it's a one-sided and distorted view. Because of his pain, he's unable to see the goodness of life and the blessings of God's grace. We should not fall into the trap of Job's pessimism, nor should we judge Job for feeling this way. This is the kind of thinking that pain and loss produce in human lives."*

　　a. Is there someone in your life who tends toward the "pit of pessimism"? Are you tempted to judge this person?

　　b. What can you think about or do to get yourself out of a judgmental mindset?

　　c. What light do the following Scriptures shed on this issue?

　　　　• Matthew 7:1–2—

　　　　• Luke 6:31—

2.　Do you ever feel like Job in this section? What are practical steps you can take to get out of the "pit of pessimism" when you are feeling like Job here? That is, tangibly and practically, how can you focus more on the goodness of life and the blessings of God's grace, even in your pain?

3.　Read Romans 5:1–5. How is it even possible that we as Christians can we rejoice in our sufferings? Stedman elaborates on this on the bottom of page 94.

## • Day 40 •
### Job 14:14–17

*Pray.*

*Practice:*  1 Thessalonians 5:11—*"Encourage one another and build each another up…"*

*Read:*  Second half of page 95 through top of page 96 ("Chapter One of the Great Story," cont.)

*Examine and Respond:*

1. In Job 14:14–17, how does Job foreshadow the sacrifice of Christ and the forgiveness we receive from Him?

2. Explore the following verses in Scripture confirming Job's "brilliant idea" that our sins will be totally forgiven. The Bible is loaded with such evidence.

   a. Psalm 103:12—

   b. Isaiah 1:18—

   c. Ephesians 1:7—

   d. Colossians 1:13–14—

   e. Hebrews 10:17

   f. 1 John 1:9—

3. How does (or should) reflecting on our being totally forgiven and shielded from the wrath of God affect our daily life?

4. How should realizing that *"that annoying Christian over there"* is also totally forgiven affect your view of and treatment of him or her?

5. Take time to thank God that He has shielded you from His wrath and removed your sins forever. May we never forget the truth and power of this reality.

# • Day 41 •
Job 14:18–22

*Pray.*

*Practice:* 2 Corinthians 1:3—*"Praise be to the God and Father of our Lord Jesus Christ, the Father of compassion and the God of all comfort..."*

*Read:* Pages 96–98 ("Chapter One of the Great Story," cont.)

*Examine and Respond:*

1. Job 14 closes with hopelessness; Job seems to be viewing life from *"the natural person's viewpoint. According to this view, all that matters is the present moment, so let's live for today"* (page 96). What is wrong with this view? What does it not take into account?

2. What is waiting for us after this life? Note what details the following verses provide.

   a. 1 Corinthians 15:51–54—

   b. 1 Peter 1:3–5—

   c. Revelation 7:16–17—

3. Scripture provides ample insight into how our view of the glory that awaits us should affect our daily living. Read each Scripture below, and then write beside it your answer to the question, *"In light of this Scripture, how should I live?"*

   a. Philippians 3:12–14—

   b. Philippians 3:17–21—

   c. Colossians 3—

# • Day 42 •

*Pray.*

*Practice:*   2 Corinthians 1:3— *"Praise be to the God and Father of our Lord Jesus Christ, the Father of compassion and the God of all comfort..."*

*Read:*       Pages 99–100 (Chapter 7 Introduction)

*Examine and Respond:*

1. Why do you think William Tyndale had such a passion for making the Scriptures available to the masses? What practical difference does having Scripture make? What difference has it made in your life? Take a moment to thank God for the gift of His written Word.

2. God answered Tyndale's prayer three years after he died. *"Oops! Too late?"* God's timeline is clearly not our own. What does the Bible have to say about this?

   a. Psalm 27:14—

   b. Proverbs 3:5–6—

   c. Ecclesiastes 3:1—

   d. Isaiah 55:8–9—

   e. Acts 1:7—

   f. 2 Peter 3:8—

   g. Can you think of a time you thought God would never answer your prayer, but He eventually did, just not in the way or timing you hoped for?

   h. What comfort can the truths of the above verses give you for daily life?

# • Day 43 •
Job 15:1–16

*Pray.*

*Practice:* 2 Corinthians 1:3—*"Praise be to the God and Father of our Lord Jesus Christ, the Father of compassion and the God of all comfort..."*

*Read:* Pages 100–102 ("The Arrogance of Eliphaz")

*Examine and Respond:*

1. What do you think of when you hear the word *pride*?

2. Look up the word *pride* in a dictionary and write its definition below.

3. *"Eliphaz has let his pride get in the way of his reason and compassion for Job"* (page 101). What does the Bible have to say about pride? A lot! Look up the following verses and note what they say about pride.

   a. Psalm 10:4—                          b. Proverbs 11:2—

   c. Proverbs 13:10—                       d. Proverbs 14:3—

   e. Proverbs 16:5—                        f. Proverbs 16:18—

   g. Obadiah 1:3—                          h. James 4:6—

4. In the verses above, you may have noticed that pride is presented as the opposite of humility or is juxtaposed to wisdom. It is perhaps more obvious how pride and humility are opposites, but in what ways is pride the opposite of *wisdom*?

5. How does pride reveal itself in human relationships? What are its potential results or effects?

6. How does pride affect a person's relationship with the Lord?

7. A handful of the 63 references to the word *pride* in Scripture (NIV) are actually positive: parents as the *pride* of their children (Proverbs 17:6), Paul's taking *pride* in his ministry and in the people of his church (Romans 11:13, 1 Corinthians 7:4), etc. What does *pride* mean in this type of context?

8. How does someone become less proud and more humble? Is this something we can work toward, or is it simply a state of heart that we need the Lord to accomplish, or something else? *"May we be strong in God's wisdom, compassion, and humility so that we never fall into the sin of Eliphaz"* (page 102).

# • Day 44 •
Job 15:17–35

*Pray.*

*Practice:* 2 Corinthians 1:3—*"Praise be to the God and Father of our Lord Jesus Christ, the Father of compassion and the God of all comfort..."*

*Read:* Pages 102–104 (" 'Blame-the-Victim' Theology")

*Examine and Respond:*

1. In this continuation of Eliphaz's speech, is there *anything* comforting? Search the passage.

2. When Jesus ascended into heaven, He promised that the Holy Spirit would come. What name did He use for the Holy Spirit? Look up John 15:26 in the King James Version.

3. In contrast, how is Satan described in Revelation 12:10?

4. Does Eliphaz seem to be speaking words from the Holy Spirit or words from Satan here? (Are they words of comfort or of accusation?)

5. Does Satan (or do any of his "servants") ever play the role of *accuser* in your life? In which areas? How can you identify when this is happening, and how can you fight it?

6. What do the following verses tell us about the comfort of the Lord?

   a. Psalm 71:21—                           b. Psalm 86:17—

   c. Isaiah 12:1—                            d. Isaiah 40:1—

   e. Isaiah 49:13—                           f. Isaiah 51:12—

   g. Isaiah 66:13—                           h. Matthew 5:4—

   i. 2 Corinthians 1:3–5—                    j. 2 Corinthians 7:6—

7. If the verses above are true of the Lord—and they are!—what should be true of those of us who follow Him and represent Him on earth? *May God give us the grace to comfort others well.*

# • Day 45 •
## Job 16

*Pray.*

*Practice:* 2 Corinthians 1:3—*"Praise be to the God and Father of our Lord Jesus Christ, the Father of compassion and the God of all comfort..."*

*Read:* Pages 104–108 ("A Prophetic Dimension")

*Examine and Respond:*

1. Do you think it is right for Job to call his friends *"miserable comforters"* in Job 16:2?

2. Is name-calling ever okay? Examine the words of Christ in the following verses:

   a. Matthew 16:23—

   b. Matthew 23:27—

   c. Are we ever justified in speaking this way, or is Jesus an exception since He is God?

3. How would you answer Job's question of his friends in Job 16:3? (What ails his friends, that they keep on arguing? What seems to be their problem? What appears to be their motivation?)

4. What does Job note in Job 16:5 that he would do if he were in the position of his friends? What encouragement and comfort do you think he would, or could, provide? What does one even say in a situation like this that could possibly bring encouragement and comfort?

5. Most people have likely had experience with someone who was not helpful in the middle of a time of suffering, good intentions or not. What is a godly response to a *"miserable comforter"*?

6. Below, record any truth you read on pages 106–108 of *Let God Be God* that stood out to you and you would like to remember.

# • Day 46 •
### Job 17

*Pray.*

*Practice:*   2 Corinthians 1:3—*"Praise be to the God and Father of our Lord Jesus Christ, the Father of compassion and the God of all comfort..."*

*Read:*   Pages 108–110 ("Hope Crumbles to Dust")

*Examine and Respond:*

1. The theme of this chapter is *"Where is my hope?"* We see Job's depth of despair hit a new low. In 2 Corinthians 10:5, what are we commanded to do with our thoughts?

2. Martin Luther once said regarding our thoughts, *"You cannot keep birds from flying over your head, but you can keep them from building a nest in your hair."* We get to choose what we focus on. What are we told to focus on in Philippians 4:8?

3. Our mind is a battlefield, and our best weapon is Scripture. In the table below are listed several of Job's laments found in Job 17. His feelings are certainly understandable. However, if he did not want to dwell there, and if he had access to the whole of Scripture, how could he have countered each lament with hope-filled Scriptural truth? Complete the table below.

| Job's Lament | Scriptural Truth |
|---|---|
| Job 17:1—*"My spirit is broken"* | Psalm 51:17— |
| Job 17:2—*"Surely there are mockers about me"* | Zephaniah 3:17— |
| Job 17:2—*"my eye dwells on their provocation"* | Hebrews 12:2— |
| Job 17:6—*"I am one before whom men spit"* | Mark 10:33–34— |
| Job 17:11—*"the desires of my heart [are broken off]"* | Psalm 37:4— |
| Job 17:12—*"The light is near to the darkness"* | 1 John 1:5— |
| Job 17:15—*"Where then is my hope?"* | Psalm 42:5— |
| Job 17:16—*"Shall we descend together into the dust?"* | Psalm 113:7— |

# • Day 47 •
Job 18

*Pray.*

*Practice:* 2 Corinthians 1:3—*"Praise be to the God and Father of our Lord Jesus Christ, the Father of compassion and the God of all comfort..."*

*Read:* Pages 110–112 ("Bildad Gets Mad")

*Examine and Respond:*

1. In Job 18, it is clear that Bildad did not appreciate Job's comments. He seems particularly ruffled that Job thinks he is *"stupid"* (Job 18:3). If he wanted to show that he is not foolish after all, but is truly wise, how would that be reflected in his speech? See Proverbs 17:28.

2. Bildad uses the recurring theme of *light and darkness* to warn Job.

   a. In what verses of Job 18 do you see Bildad focusing on this theme of *light and darkness*?

   b. What is Job's identity as a child of God? Does Bildad's warning of darkness even apply to Job? See Matthew 5:14.

3. Bildad's accusations in Job 18:7–14 involve the imagery of a trap, with a net, snare, and rope—and worse: He accuses Job of setting this trap for himself *("his own schemes throw him down,"* he notes in verse 7).

   a. Have you seen Job setting any traps for himself thus far in the book of Job, or is Bildad "full of hot air"?

   b. Who is actually responsible for the trap of misery that Job is in?

   c. Because it is easy to get bogged down in the book of Job, it is helpful periodically to go back and remember how Job is described in Job 1:1 and what God says about him in Job 1:8. Record those descriptions again here.

   d. When we are accused, lied about, and subsequently confused, two anchors to ground us are: (1) *What do I know is true about God?* and (2) *What is true of who I am in relation to God?* Make a list of key truths in each of these two categories that can help anchor you in hard and confusing situations.

## • Day 48 •
Job 19:1–27

*Pray.*

*Practice:*   2 Corinthians 1:3—*"Praise be to the God and Father of our Lord Jesus Christ, the Father of compassion and the God of all comfort..."*

*Read:*     Pages 112–115 ("My Redeemer Lives!")

*Examine and Respond:*

1. In Job 19:1, Job describes the effect of his friends' words as *"breaking him in pieces."*

   a. What would be the opposite of *"breaking [the hearer] in pieces with words"*?


   b. We—as spouses, parents, friends, and even strangers!—have great power in our tongues. How is the power of the tongue described in Proverbs 18:21?


   c. We need God's powerful help with our tongues. On Day 18 (question 5), you wrote a prayer for God's help with your words. Psalm 141:3 is another valuable daily prayer; write it below.




2. In your own words, sum up what Job says in Job 19:4.




3. In Job 19:8, Job feels as though God has caused darkness to fall on his path. He cannot see the way out of his despair. Though our path can feel dark, we need to boss our feelings around with truth. What is true about the path on which God has us, no matter how it feels?

   a. Proverbs 4:18—                                 b. Isaiah 42:16—




4. What is Job's wish as explained in Job 19:23–24? Did he get this wish?




5. Reading Job 19, we cannot help but empathize with Job. He is in deepest agony, and even those who should be on his side have turned against him. In verse 21, he begs desperately for his friends' mercy. Where are those who will *"mourn with those who mourn"*? They are nowhere to be found. Job is left with no human resource—but to what profound hope does he cling in Job 19:25–27?

# • Day 49 •

Job 19:25–27

*Pray.*

*Practice:* 2 Corinthians 1:3—*"Praise be to the God and Father of our Lord Jesus Christ, the Father of compassion and the God of all comfort..."*

*Read:* Pages 114–115 ("My Redeemer Lives!" reprise)

*Examine and Respond:*

1. Job 19:25–27 deserves our attention for a lifetime, so we will give it one more day of study. Read these verses again.

2. In times of suffering, we need to ground ourselves in what we *know* to be true. *"Never doubt in the dark what God told you in the light"* (V. Raymond Edman). Instead of darkness and confusion, what key phrase of confidence does Job state at the beginning of verse 25?

3. a. Job uses the personal pronoun *my* when referring to God as his Redeemer. What does this show you about his relationship with God and the personal, vibrant nature of his faith?

   b. David makes a similar claim in the beginning of Psalm 63:1. What does he say about God?

   c. How does this apply to you? What difference does it make that God is truly *your* God?

4. The word *Redeemer* is translated from the Hebrew *go'el*, which is used frequently in the Old Testament to refer to a "kinsman-redeemer," who had both rights and responsibilities for vindicating a family member (seen, for example, in Ruth 4:1–6). In the Old Testament, God also uses this word when He promises to redeem His people from slavery. With this understanding, what hope is Job expressing by claiming that God is his Redeemer?

5. In Job 19:26, Job acknowledges the tangible, "fleshly" nature of God's coming to earth and his own, in-the-flesh, ability in the future when he will finally see the Lord. Why is this especially poignant given the current state of Job's body? How does this relate to 2 Corinthians 4:16–18?

6. Job exclaims in Job 19:27, *"My heart faints within me!"* It is clear that his only hope—and an impassioned one, at that—is to behold his God. Would he have had this same eyes-on-the-prize excitement had he not endured so much suffering? How can you relate to this?

# • Day 50 •
Job 19:28–29

*Pray.*

*Practice:*   2 Corinthians 1:3— *"Praise be to the God and Father of our Lord Jesus Christ, the Father of compassion and the God of all comfort..."*

*Read:*   Pages 115–117 ("God Knows What He's About")

*Examine and Respond:*

1.   On page 115, how does Stedman describe one of the central themes of the book of Job?

2.   Stedman states on page 116, *"Suffering is a normal part of the human condition."*

   a. What does Jesus say in John 16:33 that confirms this truth?

   b. What else does Jesus say in John 16:33? What reason does He give for us to take heart?

   c. What does it actually mean that no matter what happens in this life, Christ has overcome the world?

3.   Job denounces his friends in Job 19:28–29 for claiming that the root of his suffering is his own fault (*"The root of the matter is found in him,"* verse 28). Job warns them in verse 29 that *"there is a judgment."* How do the following Scriptures expound on this?

   a. Matthew 12:36—

   b. 1 Corinthians 4:5—

   c. 2 Corinthians 5:10—

   d. Hebrews 9:27—

4.   Regarding a future judgment, examine Matthew 7:1–5 and Romans 14:10–13; then read John 5:24 and Romans 8:1. How do we reconcile these verses? What should our view be of a coming judgment; and how, therefore, should we live?

5.   The last five sentences on page 117 contain five key points of truth and hope. List them.

# • Day 51 •

*Pray.*

*Practice:*   1 Peter 4:19—*"Those who suffer according to God's will should commit themselves to their faithful Creator and continue to do good."*

*Read:*   Pages 119–120 (Chapter 8 Introduction and "Pharisees of Job's Day—and Ours")

*Examine and Respond:*

1. On page 119 of *Let God Be God*, we see described how a person can acknowledge deep pain and simultaneously maintain trust; the two are not mutually exclusive. David provides many examples of these coexisting truths. To explore this further, examine Psalm 42. After you have read the psalm, fill in the chart below, noting how David acknowledges both his own pain and the character of God.

| Expressions of Pain: *The Suffering that David is Enduring* | Expressions of Trust in God: *Who God Is, What He Has Done, What He Will Do* |
|---|---|
| | |

2. Recall something hard in your own life that you are going through now or have endured in the past. Reflect on how you can acknowledge the pain of this season or experience and still trust God in the middle of the hard time. Write a sentence below in the form of a prayer that recognizes these coexisting truths.

3. How does Stedman define *pharisaism* (page 120)?

4. In what area(s) of your life would it be easy to lean toward pharisaical thinking, or seeing yourself as superior because of your adherence to certain rules or rituals?

5. It has been said that Christianity is *"the great leveler."* How can remembering the truths of Ephesians 2:8–9 help us as we fight pharisaical tendencies in our own hearts?

# • Day 52 •
## Job 20

*Pray.*

*Practice:*   1 Peter 4:19—*"Those who suffer according to God's will should commit themselves to their faithful Creator and continue to do good."*

*Read:*   Pages 120–122 ("Zophar's Impassioned Speech")

*Examine and Respond:*

1. Zophar seems to appeal more to the emotions than to the intellect. What kind of trouble can people get into when their spiritual lives are led more by their emotions than by their minds?

2. Conversely, what kind of trouble can people get into if their spiritual lives neglect any emotions at the expense of their intellect?

3. Which way do you lean in your spiritual journey: emotional or intellectual? What can you do to strengthen the other side, if necessary, and grow toward a healthier balance?

4. Why do you think it is repeated and emphasized in Scripture that the greatest commandment is to love the Lord our God with all of our heart *and* mind (and soul and strength...)?

5. Zophar spends the entire chapter, Job 20, elaborating on the destiny of the wicked. Even though much of what he says is true, do you think any of it is relevant or helpful to Job?

6. An old maxim, *"Think before you speak,"* can serve as a helpful acrostic, as shown at right.

   In Job 20, we see that Zophar stops after the first qualification, "true." Even if something is true, does that mean it should be said? Scripture provides a helpful balance in Ephesians 4:15. Fill in the blank:

   *"Speaking the truth in _____"*

   God is Love (1 John 4:8), and a defining feature of His children is our love for one another (John 13:35). May that be true of us, by the power of the Holy Spirit, who equips us for every good work and every loving word from our mouths. *Lord, help us not be Zophars!*

> T: Is it true?
>
> H: Is it helpful?
>
> I: Is it inspiring?
>
> N: Is it necessary?
>
> K: Is it kind?

# • Day 53 •
Job 21

*Pray.*

*Practice:* 1 Peter 4:19—*"Those who suffer according to God's will should commit themselves to their faithful Creator and continue to do good."*

*Read:* Pages 122–127 ("Job's Reasoned Response" and "God in a Box")

*Examine and Respond:*

1. People today still echo Job's points in this chapter, from thousands of years ago. What does that tell you about human nature? Solomon dialed into this in Ecclesiastes 1:9.

2. Do you struggle with envying others who seem to get away with doing wrong or who just generally seem to have life easier, despite the way they live their lives? Where are you on the "envy spectrum"? *"For we all stumble in many ways"* (James 3:2); is envy one of your struggles?

3. How can it help us to accept the fact that, as Stedman notes on page 126, *"we live in an unfair world—a world in which the righteous suffer and the wicked prosper"*? Or, on page 125: *"There is a basic unfairness at the root of life."* How can accepting this fact actually benefit us? (Conversely, if we do not surrender to the idea of inevitable unfairness, how could that negatively affect us?) After you answer, look back at how you responded to question 5 on Day 4. Compare your responses.

4. Read Psalm 73. After reading to the end of this psalm, return to focus on verse 17.

   a. What causes David's perception of the "prosperous wicked" to change?

   b. Reflect on the ideas of true unfairness as opposed to *perceived* unfairness; unfairness viewed from a temporal versus an eternal perspective; God's discipline of those He *loves*; our limited view, seeing only slices of a bigger picture... There are entire books written about these subjects, but what are some of your initial thoughts?

5. What substitute for envy is offered in Proverbs 23:17–18? Where should we direct our zeal? What is the reason given in verse 18 for why we should not "envy sinners"?

6. Amy Carmichael, a missionary to India for 55 years, recorded this insight: *"In acceptance lieth peace."* What are practical ways to become more accepting of the apparent unfairness of life? What thought patterns are helpful in this process of acceptance? How should you actively fight the sin of envy? Make a list of your ideas, picking one to focus on making a habit. Pray for God's help in this.

# • Day 54 •
## Job 22

*Pray.*

*Practice:* 1 Peter 4:19—*"Those who suffer according to God's will should commit themselves to their faithful Creator and continue to do good."*

*Read:* Pages 128–132 ("The Third Debate Begins" and "A Childish Level of Discourse")

*Examine and Respond:*

Eliphaz's speech in this chapter is a pile of harsh and untrue allegations against Job. This is a sad but true reality for many great heroes of the faith. If this happens to us, we are in good company!

1.  Jesus set an example, that we might what? See 1 Peter 2:21.

2.  What exactly was Jesus' example? What did He do when He faced accusations? Did He defend Himself or repay the accuser? Continue reading 1 Peter 2, verses 22 and 23; then read Acts 8:32–33.

3.  What was Jesus' advice, which He also lived out?

    a. Matthew 5:11–12—

    b. Matthew 5:43–45—

4.  Have you ever been falsely accused? How did it feel? How did you react? How did the situation dissipate? What did you learn from it? What would you do differently next time? Reflect on this.

5.  We can trust God always—even when we don't feel like it, even amidst slander and lies. Of what truth are we reminded in Romans 12:19? Read this verse in the New Living Translation.

6.  If we are slandered but continue to react graciously, what is a possible end result? It is worth it! See 1 Peter 2:12.

7.  Read 1 Peter 3:8–17 and summarize the main point of the passage.

8.  No matter what false allegations are hurled our way, we are called to the life of 1 Peter 4:19, which is what?

# • Day 55 •
## Job 23

*Pray.*

*Practice:*   1 Peter 4:19—*"Those who suffer according to God's will should commit themselves to their faithful Creator and continue to do good."*

*Read:*   Pages 132–134 ("The First Question")

*Examine and Respond:*

1.   How does Job state what he is longing for in Job 23:3? Restate it in your own words.

2.   Despite how he feels, what does Job say in Job 23:6–7 that expresses confidence in God?

3.   In Job 23:8–9, Job returns to an expression of despair. He feels like God is nowhere in sight.

   a. Can you relate? When have you felt unable to find or connect to God?

   b. What has gotten you through those dark times?

4.   a. What amazing statement of faith does Job say in Job 23:10? Write it by memory if possible.

   b. Elaborate on what Job means by this. Stedman has his own version on page 133, but how would you explain it in your own words, about your own life? Write this as your own personal statement of faith through suffering.

5.   Once again, at the end of this chapter, Job returns to an acknowledgement of his feelings. What does he say he feels toward God in Job 23:15–16?

6.   Job will not let his feelings get in the way of pursuing communication with God, even when God feels far off. How do you see this expressed in Job 23:17? What can you learn from this?

*Pray.*

*Practice:* 1 Peter 4:19—*"Those who suffer according to God's will should commit themselves to their faithful Creator and continue to do good."*

*Read:* Pages 134–137 ("The Second Question")

*Examine and Respond:*

1. Job's previous question had to do with the apparent *absence* of God; here, he questions the apparent *silence* of God—in particular, why God does not judge at all, judge more, or judge sooner. How does Job phrase this issue in the following verses?

   a. Job 24:1—

   b. Job 24:12—

2. What do we learn from the Apostle Paul in Romans 2:4 about why God sometimes appears too kind, tolerant, and patient?

3. What light did Peter shed on this idea? What reasons does he give for God's apparent "slowness"? See 2 Peter 3:9.

4. Every one of us has a life that depends wholly on the grace, mercy, and patience of God. His mercy exceeds that of any human on earth. What do we learn about God's mercy in the verses below?

   a. 2 Samuel 24:14—                    b. Nehemiah 9:31—

   c. Psalm 25:6—                         d. Isaiah 55:7—

5. As recipients of God's mercy, we are to lavish it on others in response. What does Matthew 5:7 have to say about this?

6. What exactly *is* mercy? Look it up in a dictionary and write the definition below. Then write a list of practical ways for you to show more mercy to others. God will help you in this endeavor! This is His will for you.

# • Day 57 •
## Job 25

*Pray.*

*Practice:* 1 Peter 4:19—*"Those who suffer according to God's will should commit themselves to their faithful Creator and continue to do good."*

*Read:* Pages 137–138 ("You Are Not a 'Worm'!")

*Examine and Respond:*

1. Bildad and Job's other friends serve as a good reminder that even if words are true in the literal sense, they can be communicated with the wrong motive, tone, emphasis, or audience: with motives of condemnation instead of comfort; harshly instead of kindly; emphasizing God's justice over His love and mercy; addressing "big, bad sinners" rather than children of God preciously loved and highly esteemed by Him. We see this in churches, in families, in friendships; no one is immune. We always must compare a human's words (including our own!) to what we know of the character and words of God before we accept them as truth. With that in mind, summarize what Bildad says in each verse listed below and then place a symbol or note in the respective box on the right to reflect your opinion about what he says.

| *Verse* | *Fully true?* | *Right motive?* | *Kind tone?* | *Seems balanced?* | *Appropriate audience?* |
|---|---|---|---|---|---|
| Job 25:2— | | | | | |
| Job 25:3— | | | | | |
| Job 25:4— | | | | | |
| Job 25:5— | | | | | |
| Job 26:6— | | | | | |

2. Bildad refers to humans as *"maggots"* and *"worms"* (Job 25:6), but this is certainly not in line with what we know of God and His opinion of us. What does the Bible say about our identity and worth before God?

   a. Genesis 1:27—                                   b. 1 Peter 2:9—



   c. 1 John 3:1–2—



3. Why is an accurate sense of identity important in one's daily life? Why does it matter? How does it manifest itself?

## • Day 58 •
Job 26

*Pray.*

*Practice:*   1 Peter 4:19—*"Those who suffer according to God's will should commit themselves to their faithful Creator and continue to do good."*

*Read:*   Pages 138–141 ("The Grand Perhaps")

*Examine and Respond:*

1. What sarcasm or irony appears in Job 26:2–4?

2. After Job "gets his sassies out," he focuses on the greatness of God. Although his friends used thoughts of God's greatness to threaten Job and "put him in his place," Job seems to view God's greatness as something awe-inspiring. How do human perceptions of God's greatness depend on one's perceived standing before and relationship with God? How do *you* feel when you reflect on the unparalleled power of God?

3. What do we see in Job 26:14 that hints at Job's surrendering to the idea of God's understanding surpassing his own? This idea is key in our acceptance of suffering.

4. *"Job's sufferings have magnified his image of God"* (page 140). When have you seen this occur in your own life?

5. In the depths of suffering, it is easy to think that whatever spiritual gains to be had are absolutely not worth it. We would rather not suffer, even if the suffering means growth of our souls. However, we are told repeatedly in Scripture that knowing God and growing our faith *are* worth whatever pain is necessary. How is this confirmed in the following verses?

    a. Philippians 3:7–8—

    b. 1 Peter 1:6–7—

*"Run! Run! Run with perseverance the race that is set before you. IT IS WORTH IT ALL."*
-The Great Cloud of Witnesses (Hebrews 12:1)

# • Day 59 •

*Pray.*

*Practice:*  1 Peter 4:19—*"Those who suffer according to God's will should commit themselves to their faithful Creator and continue to do good."*

*Read:*  Pages 143–144 (Chapter 9 Introduction)

*Examine and Respond:*

1.  Saints throughout history can be a tremendous source of insight, inspiration, and strength to us as we journey through this life. The writer of Hebrews devotes chapter 11 to listing saints who have walked before us and demonstrated great faith. What should their example inspire us to do? Read Hebrews 12:1–3. In the margins of this page, list everything you see in these verses about how we should live in light of those who have faithfully gone before us.

2.  In Polycarp's last moments of suffering, he said, *"The will of God be done"* (page 143). What do we know about God's will from Scripture?

    a. God's will is _____ than our will. (Luke 22:42)

    b. God's will is _____, _____, and _____. (Romans 12:2)

    c. It is God's will that we should be _____. (1 Thessalonians 4:3)

    d. It is God's will for us to give _____ in all circumstances. (1 Thessalonians 5:18)

3.  Which of the above verses about the will of God hits home most for you?

4.  At the end of a believer's life, he or she can truthfully say with Polycarp that God *"has never done me any harm. How can I curse my King, the one who saved me?"* (page 143). How do the following verses reflect this truth?

    a. Psalm 13:6—                    b. Psalm 116:7—

    c. What did Paul say at the end of his life? See 2 Timothy 4:6–8.

5.  How could Polycarp—or how could we—say that it is a *privilege* to *"drink the cup of Christ's sufferings"* (page 144)?

# • Day 60 •
## Job 27

*Pray.*

*Practice:*    1 Peter 4:19— *"Those who suffer according to God's will should commit themselves to their faithful Creator and continue to do good."*

*Read:*    Pages 144–146 ("An Unyielding Stance")

*Examine and Respond:*

1.  In this chapter, Job stands firm. Despite the continual battering by his friends in his most vulnerable state, Job will not give in and confess to what he believes is wrong. In what verse of Job 27 do you see this resoluteness most clearly?

2.  In the words of Stedman on page 145, *"You have to admire the spirit of a man who is determined to tell the truth, even if it costs him everything."* Where in Scripture are we taught to have such determination? Make notes beside the verses listed below.

    a. Daniel 1:8—                             b. Isaiah 50:7—

    c. Luke 21:19—                             d. 1 Corinthians 15:58—

    e. 1 Corinthians 16:13—                    f. 2 Thessalonians 3:13—

    g. James 5:8—

3.  Clearly, we are Christians are called to stand firm. But how can we do this? What is the source of this strength? See 2 Corinthians 1:21–22.

4.  Is there an area of your life where you are feeling tempted or pressured to give in or give up? Identify this. Then write a prayer of resolution, voicing to God your determination to stand firm in this area of struggle. *He is able to do immeasurably more than all we ask or imagine, according to His power that is at work in us!* (Ephesians 3:20)

# • Day 61 •
Job 28

*Pray.*

*Practice:* Psalm 23:4 (ESV)—*"Even though I walk through the valley of the shadow of death, I will fear no evil, for You are with me..."*

*Read:* Pages 147–151 ("The Treasures of Wisdom" and "The Answers to the Riddles of Life")

*Examine and Respond:*

1. The first eleven verses of Job 28 *"poetically picture the quest for wisdom as a search for hidden treasure"* (page 147). How would you describe wisdom? What is it, and why is it valuable?

2. Read 1 Kings 3. When the Lord tells Solomon to ask him for anything he wants, Solomon asks for wisdom. How does Solomon describe wisdom in 1 Kings 3:9?

3. How would Solomon's description of wisdom apply to you today? Solomon needed it for governing his people. What are your current needs for wisdom?

4. We do not know how all prayers will be answered, but what do we know about prayers for wisdom? See James 1:5.

5. Job 28's discussion of wisdom may sound familiar; the books of wisdom literature in Scripture share many common themes. Examine some parallels below.

   a. Read the following verses: Proverbs 4:7, Proverbs 9:10, Proverbs 16:16, and Psalm 111:10.

   b. How do Proverbs 9:10 and Psalm 111:10 echo Job 28:28?

6. The New Testament also has much to say about wisdom. Look up the following verses.

   a. James 3:13—          b. James 3:17—          c. Colossians 4:5–6—

   d. In light of these verses, how would you summarize what wisdom looks like in daily life?

7. How do we acquire wisdom? If we are told in Scripture to do whatever it takes to get it, what does that actually mean? What should we do? What habits should we cultivate? Record any needs, intentions, and prayers for wisdom in the margins of this page. Don't forget James 1:5 (question 4)!

# • Day 62 •
## Job 29

*Pray.*

*Practice:* Psalm 23:4 (ESV)—*"Even though I walk through the valley of the shadow of death, I will fear no evil, for You are with me..."*

*Read:* Pages 151–153 ("The Good Old Days")

*Examine and Respond:*

1. In this chapter of Job, we see Job—very understandably—longing for "the good old days." What is the first loss that Job grieves (Job 29:2–5)? What does the fact that this is first show us about Job?

2. In the following verses, how does Job describe his relationship with God?

   a. Job 29:2—                          b. Job 29:3—

   c. Job 29:4—                          d. Job 29:5—

3. What does Solomon say in Ecclesiastes 7:10, and what does it have to do with this chapter of Job? Do you agree with Solomon?

4. Are you prone to idealizing "the good old days"? When *can* it be useful to reflect on the past?

5. During a dark or dry time, how can it be helpful to recall what has been true in the past about your relationship with God? See Psalm 143:5.

6. How would you summarize what Job's reputation used to be in Job 29:6–11?

7. From the previous verses, it could be assumed that people showed Job respect because of his wealth or status, but in Job 29:12–25 we see a touching explanation of the causes to which, and the people to whom, Job was devoted.

   a. Note some of the admirable things that Job did. How does Job live out what James describes as *"true religion"* in James 1:27?

   b. How can you, like Job, better live out James 1:27?

# • Day 63 •
## Job 30

*Pray.*

*Practice:*   Psalm 23:4 (ESV)—*"Even though I walk through the valley of the shadow of death, I will fear no evil, for You are with me..."*

*Read:*   Pages 153–156 ("The Heaviest Burden of All")

*Examine and Respond:*

1. Job's past is juxtaposed with his current situation. How do men treat him now compared to how people used to treat him? He devotes the first fifteen verses of chapter 30 to explaining this, but verse 1 is a good sum-up. Note what it says below.

2. In Job 30:16, Job begins describing his personal and internal anguish. In verses 19 through 21 comes the greatest grief of all. What is it?

3. In the following verses, what does Job say that God has done to him? Restate each verse in your own words.

    a. Job 30:11—

    b. Job 30:19—

    c. Job 30:21–22—

4. What is the difference between what Job is saying about God and actually *cursing* God? There is a fine line, but he does not cross it. Where is that line?

5. In Job 30:25, how does Job describe his reaction to others who are suffering? How does that contrast with how his friends have treated him?

6. The Lord often ministers to our needs by using other people to help us, but Jesus Himself knew that people cannot always be relied on. How is this explained in John 2:25?

7. We have one alone whom we can count on 100% of the time. Write out Psalm 23:4 in the space below. *Thank You, Lord, that You are always with me.*

# • Day 64 •
### Job 31:1–12

*Pray.*

*Practice:*   Psalm 23:4 (ESV)—*"Even though I walk through the valley of the shadow of death, I will fear no evil, for You are with me..."*

*Read:*    Pages 156–157 (first part of "Job's Final Defense")

*Examine and Respond:*

1. In this chapter, Job 31, we see Job examining his life and finding no sin that would merit the suffering he is enduring. In Job 31:1, he notes, *"I have made a covenant with my eyes."* There is much wisdom in this brief statement. Note that Job is not committed only to avoiding the flagrant action of adultery, but he "nips it in the bud" and stops himself early in the path along that sin. Also note that he has not merely "tried to do better"; instead, he uses strong words to express his absolute commitment to purity. May we do the same?

   a. Think of a sin that you find yourself struggling with or know you are prone to.


   b. Trace that sin back. With what initial thoughts or actions does it begin?


   c. Emulate Job and devote yourself to stopping sin in its tracks in its earliest stage. God gives us the strength, but we also need to do our part: commit and carry out.


2. What statement does Job make about God in Job 31:4?


3. How is this idea confirmed in other parts of Scripture?

   a. Genesis 28:15—

   b. Deuteronomy 32:10—

   c. Psalm 32:8—

   d. Psalm 121:8—

   e. Matthew 6:4—


4. If it is true that God sees our ways and numbers all our steps—and it is!—what difference does that, should that, *will* that make for you *today*?

# • Day 65 •
Job 31:13–40

*Pray.*

*Practice:*    Psalm 23:4 (ESV)—*"Even though I walk through the valley of the shadow of death, I will fear no evil, for You are with me..."*

*Read:*    Pages 157–160 (finishing "Job's Final Defense")

*Examine and Respond:*

1.  As a man of great wealth, Job had many people working for him. Culturally, it would have been expected for him to think of himself as superior to them. However, what does Job say in Job 31:13–23 that leads us to believe that he did *not* consider himself to be more important?

2.  What truth in Job 31:15 provides the basis for our never seeing ourselves as more important than anyone else, and for treating others as we would like to be treated? How is this idea reinforced in Genesis 1:27?

3.  We have much to learn from Job's self-assessment in this chapter. Complete the table below as a summary, extension, and application of this portion of Job.

| Verses | Summary: Area Job Addresses | Extension: Elsewhere in Scripture | Application: My Takeaways |
|---|---|---|---|
| Job 31:13–23 | Treating the poor/needy favorably | Proverbs 19:17— | |
| Job 31:24–28 | Not trusting in his wealth | 1 Timothy 6:17— | |
| Job 31:29–30 | Showing kindness to his enemies | Matthew 5:44— | |
| Job 31:31–32 | Practicing generous hospitality | Romans 12:13 and Hebrews 13:2— | |
| Job 31:33–37 | Avoiding secret sins and living with integrity | Proverbs 11:3 and 2 Corinthians 1:12— | |
| Job 31:38–40 | Faithfully stewarding the land | Genesis 1:26–29 and Genesis 2:15— | |

4.  Which area in the chart above do you find most compelling, inspiring, or imitable? Explain.

# • Day 66 •

*Pray.*

*Practice:*   Psalm 23:4 (ESV)— *"Even though I walk through the valley of the shadow of death, I will fear no evil, for You are with me..."*

*Read:*   Pages 160–162 ("The Greatest Lesson of the Book of Job")

*Examine and Respond:*

1.  Stedman makes many points on page 160 that we would do well to take to heart. Which ones are most impactful to you?

2.  Stedman notes on page 160 that *"It's no sin to question God. He welcomes our questions and is patient with our limitations."* What examples can you recall from Jesus' time on earth and His interactions with people that support this idea?

3.  What does it mean to be *"poor in spirit"* (Matthew 5:3)?

4.  Part of saving faith is repentance, and part of repentance is a deep awareness of and sorrow over one's sin. What place does self-defense have in this process?

5.  Job's friends appear to think of repentance as a way to gain merit from God. There seems to be no room in their theology for love and favor from God toward the godless while they are still sinners. It seems that Job, too, feels the need to justify himself before God. What truths about this issue do we find in the following verses?

    a. Romans 5:6–8—

    b. Philippians 3:7–9—

    We do not need to defend ourselves or "clean ourselves up" before coming to God. The words of the hymn at right can be our prayer today, and every day. *Just as I am, without one plea... O Lamb of God, I come.*

> Just as I am, without one plea
> But that Thy blood was shed for me
> And that Thou bid'st me come to Thee
> O Lamb of God, I come! I come.
>
> Just as I am, though tossed about
> With many a conflict, many a doubt
> Fighting and fears within without
> O Lamb of God, I come, I come.
>
> Just as I am, and waiting not
> to rid my soul of one dark blot
> to Thee whose blood can cleanse each spot
> O Lamb of God, I come, I come.
>
> Just as I am, poor, wretched, blind
> Sight, riches, healing of the mind
> Yea, all I need, in Thee to find
> O Lamb of God, I come, I come!
>
> Just as I am, Thou wilt receive
> Wilt welcome, pardon, cleanse, relieve
> Because Thy promise I believe
> O Lamb of God, I come, I come!
>
> - Charlotte Elliott, 1835

# • Day 67 •
Job 32:1–5

*Pray.*

*Practice:*   Psalm 23:4 (ESV)—*"Even though I walk through the valley of the shadow of death, I will fear no evil, for You are with me..."*

*Read:*   Page 163 (Chapter 10 Introduction)

*Examine and Respond:*

1. In Job 32:1, Job's three friends having nothing more to say. What is their reason for this?

2. Job's friends stop speaking to Job because they consider him *"righteous in his own eyes."*

   a. From the beginning of the book of Job, who else do we know considers Job righteous?

   b. Whose opinion counts more—God's or that of Job's friends?

   c. Whose favorable opinion do you find yourself striving for the most? Why?

   d. The phrase *"an audience of one"* can be helpful in many of life's situations. Never will *everyone* understand us, like us, or approve of the way we live. How do the following verses encourage us to strive to please God and God alone?

   • Galatians 1:10—          • Ephesians 6:7—          • Colossians 3:23–24—

3. Unexpectedly, a young man named Elihu takes a turn to speak. (We did not even know he existed until now!) How does knowing that others have been present during this time affect your view of Job's situation?

4. From the first five verses of Job 32, we see that Elihu seems to have been bottling some anger.

   a. Why is Elihu angry with Job?          b. Why is Elihu angry with Job's three friends?

   c. Is Elihu wrong to feel angry? Is it *ever* wrong to feel angry?

   d. What evidence in Job 32:4 do we see that despite feeling angry, Elihu is respectful and controlled? What can we learn from this?

# • Day 68 •
Job 32:6–10

*Pray.*

*Practice:*    Psalm 23:4 (ESV)—*"Even though I walk through the valley of the shadow of death, I will fear no evil, for You are with me..."*

*Read:*    Pages 164–166 ("Elihu—A Misunderstood Young Man")

*Examine and Respond:*

1. What can we learn from Elihu's attitude as revealed in Job 32:7?


2. Where else in Scripture is this idea repeated?

   a. Leviticus 19:32—                          b. Deuteronomy 32:7—


   c. Proverbs 23:22—                           d. 1 Timothy 5:1—


3. Do you have older people in your life whom you respect and from whom you can glean wisdom? Who are they, and how do they show themselves to be wise? Try to be in contact with one of those people this week, seek to learn from him/her, and write down what you learn. Most of us are "the older one" to others, too; may we endeavor to make ourselves available to them.


4. In Job 32:8–9, Elihu shifts from acknowledging that his elders are likely wiser than he is to the idea that it is not inherent in age to be wise. What does he say actually makes a man wise, rather than age? See verse 8.


5. How does Paul's encouragement to young Timothy in 1 Timothy 4:12 relate to Elihu's idea that perhaps the young have something wise to offer too?


6. How does Ecclesiastes 4:13 build upon this idea as well?


7. Perhaps in this section, what we learn most from Elihu is that we need to listen to older people who may be wiser than we are, and we need to listen to younger people too. In essence, we need to *listen* to those who fear the Lord, no matter what their age. What is one area of listening you want to improve on this week?

# • Day 69 •
Job 32:11–22

*Pray.*

*Practice:* Psalm 23:4 (ESV)—*"Even though I walk through the valley of the shadow of death, I will fear no evil, for You are with me..."*

*Read:* Pages 166–168 ("An Old Testament Version of John the Baptist" and "Compelled by the Spirit")

*Examine and Respond:*

1. In this portion of chapter 32, Elihu continues to speak. In verse 18, he says that he is *"full of words,"* but that *"the spirit within me constrains me"* (ESV). The NIV translates this as *"the spirit within me compels me,"* and the NLT states, *"the spirit within me urges me on."* Do you think Elihu is referring to his own spirit, the Holy Spirit, his conscience, or something else? Has a similar experience ever happened to you?

2. Elihu says in Job 32:20 that he *"must speak"*—but the motive he provides is so that he can personally *"find relief."* Can you relate to this, either as someone to whom someone else has vented or as someone who finds it helpful to vent? Give an example.

3. Is *"finding relief"* a good or bad motivation for speaking up, or does it depend on the situation? Explain.

4. If we are bursting with things to say, we are wise to hold our tongues, as Elihu did for so long. If we hold our tongues and still feel as though we will burst, what are good outlets for us to "let off steam" if the person we want to "burst to" will not benefit from what we have to say?

5. In Job 32:21, Elihu declares a commitment not to *"show partiality to any man or use flattery toward any person."* Partiality and flattery are mentioned often throughout Scripture, and the Bible makes clear God's hatred of both. Have you ever made a personal commitment about how you will treat or speak about other people? If so, what is that commitment, and how are you doing in carrying it out? If you have never made such a commitment, now is a good time. Ponder your commitment, record it in the space below, and then pray that God will help you carry it out. He will!

# • Day 70 •
Job 33:1–14

*Pray.*

*Practice:*  Psalm 23:4 (ESV)—*"Even though I walk through the valley of the shadow of death, I will fear no evil, for You are with me..."*

*Read:*  Pages 168–171 ("A Refreshing Difference in Tone")

*Examine and Respond:*

1. What tone do you sense from Elihu in Job 33:1–4?

2. In Job 33:6, what of what Elihu says do you believe is true, and what do you think could be Elihu's misrepresentation of reality?

3. Write Job 33:7 in your own words. What does this verse show us about Elihu?

4. Repeatedly in Scripture we hear the command, *"Don't be afraid."* We hear it from angels, from our Heavenly Father, and from Christ when He was on earth. In Job 33:7, Elihu is essentially saying just that—*"Job, don't be afraid. I'm not here to hurt you"*—reassuring Job before he dives into his speech that Job does not need to fear him or what he is about to say. Below are listed a few examples of where we see this idea in other parts of Scripture. Make notes beside each verse.

| God the Father | Isaiah 41:10— | |
|---|---|---|
| God the Son | Matthew 10:31— | Matthew 14:27— |
| | Mark 5:36— | Mark 6:50— |
| | Luke 12:7— | John 6:20— |
| God's Messengers | Luke 1:11–13— | Luke 1:30— |

5. Take a moment to consider how this oft-repeated Scriptural exhortation of *"Don't be afraid"* could be helpful for you to remember as you fight your own fears, or helpful for you as you encourage someone else who may need those words right now.


Isaiah 7:4—*"Be careful, keep calm, and don't be afraid. Do not lose heart..."*

# • Day 71 •
### Job 33:15–22

*Pray.*

*Practice:* Job 36:5 (NLT)—*"God is mighty, but He does not despise anyone! He is mighty in both power and understanding."*

*Read:* Pages 171–172 ("God Speaks Through Our Dreams and Our Pain")

*Examine and Respond:*

1. Elihu's premise as he speaks to Job is that God *does* speak, but not in ways that people always immediately understand. Have you ever realized after the fact that God had been speaking to you, but you either chose not to listen or had not recognized it at the time?

2. Elihu notes that one way God speaks is through dreams and visions. Has this ever been the case for you?

3. In Job 33:16, Elihu states that the dreams God allows people to have may terrify them, but ultimately (verses 17–18), why does God allow them? In the words of C.S. Lewis, perhaps they are given as a *"severe mercy."*

4. In Job 33:19–22, Elihu provides the second way he can think of that God speaks, which is through pain. Has God ever "shouted at you" through your pain?

5. We can agree with Elihu that: (1) God does speak to us; (2) often, we do not recognize it; and (3) at times He speaks through dreams, visions, or suffering—but is any of this relevant to Job? Rewind to the beginning of this book. Is God's intent in allowing Job to suffer actually to sanctify Job, to turn him aside from sin, to *"keep back his soul from the pit"*?

6. Elihu is a controversial figure in theological circles. Some commentators see him as full of helpful counsel preparing Job for God's coming words, like John the Baptist; others interpret his speeches as "more of the same": false condemnations like those of Job's other friends. Stedman presents Elihu in a favorable light; you will come to your own conclusion. It is likely that, like most people, Elihu has some valuable things to say and some that are not quite true or beneficial. Could Elihu perhaps be speaking general truth that is not actually helpful, inspiring, necessary, or kind to Job in this section? What do you think?

7. How should we determine if the truth we have in our minds will be helpful—even if hard—for the hearer? What thought process should we go through when we are trying to decide whether those hard-to-hear words are worth saying, according to the filter of Ephesians 4:29?

# • Day 72 •
Job 33:23–25

*Pray.*

*Practice:* Job 36:5 (NLT)—*"God is mighty, but He does not despise anyone! He is mighty in both power and understanding."*

*Read:* Pages 173–175 ("The Gospel According to Elihu")

*Examine and Respond:*

1. Look up the word "mediator" in a dictionary. Summarize the definition below.

2. In what ways did Elihu imagine that a mediator would help Job?

3. Now look up the word "ransom" in a dictionary. Summarize the definition below.

4. In Job 33:24, Elihu's hypothetical mediator is described as merciful, and the mediator claims, *"I have found a ransom."* Jesus, however, did not just *find* a ransom... Rather, what did Jesus do? See Mark 10:45.

5. What hope does Elihu describe in Job 33:25?

6. How is the hope expressed in Job 33:25 *ours* when the Lord causes us to be "born again"?

7. As we explored on Day 57, an accurate sense of identity is crucial in the Christian life. Therefore, it is worth exploring what exactly it means to be "born again"—because as followers of Christ, this is what we are. Read the following verses, jotting notes beside each.

   a. John 3:3, 7—                              b. 1 Peter 1:23—

   c. 2 Corinthians 5:17—                       d. Galatians 6:15—

8. In light of the above Scriptures, explain what it means to be "born again."

9. Reflect on ways in which God has truly made you a new creation, and thank Him for this wonderful transformation He has done in your heart. It is easy to forget about this miracle unless we intentionally take time to stop, remember, and give thanks.

# • Day 73 •
Job 33:26–33

*Pray.*

*Practice:*  Job 36:5 (NLT)—*"God is mighty, but He does not despise anyone! He is mighty in both power and understanding."*

*Read:*  Page 175 ("The Silence of Job")

*Examine and Respond:*

1. Job 33:26 states, *"Then man prays to God, and He accepts him..."* This is a miracle that demonstrates the incredible heart of our Father. How do the following verses echo the same truth?

    a. Isaiah 44:22—                              b. Isaiah 55:7—


    c. Jeremiah 24:7—                            d. John 6:37—


2. In Job 33:28, how does Elihu speak exactly to what Job has been feeling? God has the solution to our every need. As long as there is God, there is hope—specific hope for each specific situation.


3. How does Elihu describe the patience and mercy of God in Job 33:29?


4. If "God is Love," it could also be said that "God is Patience." It is the essence of who He is. Psalm 86:15, 103:8, and 145:8 are just a few examples of this description of God. Read these verses, and then reflect: When has God shown incredible patience toward you, giving you many chances to come back to right relationship and right living?


5. How does Elihu remind Job in Job 33:32 that he is on his side, trying to help him? When and why is this verbal reminder important in human relationships? Are there people in your life now who may need your gentle reminder that you are on their side?

# • Day 74 •
Job 34:1–4

*Pray.*

*Practice:*  Job 36:5 (NLT)—*"God is mighty, but He does not despise anyone! He is mighty in both power and understanding."*

*Read:*  Page 177–178 (Chapter 11 Introduction)

*Examine and Respond:*

1.  In the opening of Job 34, Elihu summons his hearers to test what is true, to figure out what is good.

    a. How does God give the same invitation in Isaiah 1:18?

    b. How does Paul invite his hearers to do the same? See 1 Corinthians 10:15.

2.  In Job 34:3, Elihu compares our palates, tasting food, to our ears, testing words.

    a. Do your ears naturally test what they hear? Where are you on the "skeptic scale"?

    b. What people or sources of information that are a regular part of your life do you need to test most carefully what you hear or read from them?

    c. Psychologically, how is a person affected by repeated inputs with little questioning? How does this make you want to be extra protective of what enters your ears?

3.  In Job 34:4 in the ESV, Elihu states, *"Let us choose what is right."* That sounds like a familiar refrain our culture that hails relative truth. Is this what Elihu means by *"Let us choose what is right"*? Explain in your own words what he means.

4.  *"Let us know among ourselves what is good,"* says Elihu in Job 34:4. This begs for Micah 6:8, which tells us, *"He has shown you, O man, what is good..."* What *is* good, according to Micah 6:8? God has shown us!

# • Day 75 •
Job 34:5–9

*Pray.*

*Practice:*   Job 36:5 (NLT)—*"God is mighty, but He does not despise anyone! He is mighty in both power and understanding."*

*Read:*   Page 178–179 ("Elihu Confronts Job's Flawed View of God")

*Examine and Respond:*

1.  Elihu attempts to sum up Job's words and attitudes toward God in Job 34:5–6. Do you agree with his summary?

2.  In Job 34:7–9, Elihu describes his perception of those with whom Job keeps company. How well does Elihu's description match reality? What do you remember about those to whom Job devoted his time and resources?

3.  In Job 34:9, Elihu essentially claims that Job does not delight in God. What has Job actually said about this? See Job 23:12.

4.  Now that we have seen some things Elihu says that are not true, should we dismiss his speech completely or simply continue to filter it? Is there ever anyone whose words and opinions we can 100% trust? Conversely, is there ever anyone whose words we can entirely dismiss?

5.  Although in Job 34:9, Elihu claims that Job said, *"It profits a man nothing that he should take delight in God,"* we who are followers of God know that taking delight in God is the greatest joy there is; everything else comes up empty. Who else in Scripture revels in his delight in the Lord? Write notes beside the verses below.

    a. Psalm 43:4—                                        b. Isaiah 61:10—

6.  It is to our own profit to delight in the God who delights in us. Practically, what would it look like in your life to *delight* in God more? Is there anything you can do more (or do less?) to foster this delight?

*Pray.*

*Practice:* Job 36:5 (NLT)—*"God is mighty, but He does not despise anyone! He is mighty in both power and understanding."*

*Read:* Page 179–181 ("Why God Cannot Be Unfair")

*Examine and Respond:*

1. In Job 34:10, Elihu speaks foundational truth about God. Reread that verse.

   a. What does Elihu state in this verse about God's character?

   b. In Deuteronomy 32:4, how does Moses phrase the same truth?

   c. Why is the truth that *God does no wrong* important for us to remember in times of suffering?

2. Do you agree with Elihu's assertion in Job 34:11? In what ways is his statement true, and what exceptions do you note? Examine this issue below.

   a. In agreement with Elihu, among other verses in Scripture, are the first part of Deuteronomy 32:35 and Jeremiah 17:10. Note here what these verses say.

   b. In potential disagreement with Elihu are many other verses, including Psalm 103:10 and Micah 7:18. What do David and Micah say in these verses?

   c. How do we reconcile these seemingly conflicting ideas?

3. Elihu explains that humans tend to be partial and unjust, yet God never is; thus, God is accountable to no human. Why is this important for us to keep in mind? What difference does it make in our daily lives?

# • Day 77 •
Job 34:21–37

*Pray.*

*Practice:*  Job 36:5 (NLT)—*"God is mighty, but He does not despise anyone! He is mighty in both power and understanding."*

*Read:*  Page 181–185 ("Righteousness Like Filthy Rags")

*Examine and Respond:*

1.  a. How would you summarize Job 34:21–22 in one sentence?


    b. How is this idea reiterated in Psalm 139:7–12?


    c. How would an unbeliever's response to the truth that *God Always Sees and I Cannot Hide* compare to a believer's?


    d. How does this truth affect you? Practically, what difference does it make in your life?



2.  a. What does Job 34:28 tell us about God?


    b. How does that truth apply to you?



3.  Stedman notes on page 183: *"Our Lord is not in the business of reforming people. He's in the business of renewing people. He doesn't want to make us better; He wants to make us new. God desires our repentance and relationship, not reform."* Do you agree?

    a. What does 2 Corinthians 5:17 state that confirms Stedman's opinion?


    b. Could it be that this is not an *"either/or"* issue, but rather a *"first/and also"* issue? That is, could it be that after God renews His children, He works with them to help reform them? How does 2 Corinthians 7:1 shed light on this?



4.  Stedman again takes a favorable view of Elihu in this chapter. What do *you* think about Elihu's claims and tone at the end of Job 34?

# • Day 78 •
## Job 35

*Pray.*

*Practice:*  Job 36:5 (NLT)—*"God is mighty, but He does not despise anyone! He is mighty in both power and understanding."*

*Read:*  Page 185–187 ("Why God is Sometimes Silent")

*Examine and Respond:*

1.  In Job 35:2–3, Elihu summarizes what he takes as Job's point of view, which is that the righteous are no better off than the wicked, so he might as well not have tried to live such an upright life!

    a. Have you ever wondered this about your own life? If so, what was your process of coming back to the truth that serving God is always the best way to go?

    b. Why does God give us commands? See Deuteronomy 10:13.

2.  In Job 34:5–8, Elihu essentially says that God is unfazed either by Job's sins or by his good works; they don't affect Him, just other humans. What do other Scriptures say about this?

    a. How is God affected by the sins of humankind in Genesis 6:6?

    b. How is God affected by good works in Hebrews 13:16?

    c. With the above Scriptures in mind, how do you think the way you live affects God?

    d. Does your answer in (c) lead you to see reassess anything about the way you are living?

3.  In Job 35:9–16, Elihu explains that God does not answer people because they cry out simply for their own relief and not out of any delight in Him or desire to know Him more.

    a. How does James touch on this idea in James 4:3?

    b. Is it *wrong* to pray simply for a relief from pain?

    c. What would be an "ideal" prayer in a time of deep suffering, one that God might be pleased to hear?

# • Day 79 •
Job 36:1–21

*Pray.*

*Practice:* Job 36:5 (NLT)— *"God is mighty, but He does not despise anyone! He is mighty in both power and understanding."*

*Read:* Page 187–189 ("The Glory of God Revealed")

*Examine and Respond:*

1. In Job 36:1–4, Elihu claims to be speaking from divine authority. In that context, what do you think he means by the last part of verse 4?

2. God is *perfect in knowledge*.

   a. How does this fact help us in our suffering?

   b. How does this fact help us interpret disastrous world events?

   c. How does this fact help us in day-to-day life?

3. Job 36:5 provides a true and heartening description of God: Though He is mighty in power and understanding, He does not despise us. In fact, quite the opposite, and quite unfathomably, He *delights* in us! Read, jot notes beneath, and take heart from the verses below.

   a. Zephaniah 3:17—      b. Psalm 18:19—      c. Psalm 149:4—

4. Job 36:15 states a key Biblical principle. In the New Living Translation, this verse reads, *"But by means of their suffering, He rescues those who suffer. For He gets their attention through adversity."*

   a. Restate this verse in your own words.

   b. Has this ever been true in your life?

   c. What are some truths that God may want to "open our ears to" through our suffering?

5. Elihu's exhortation in Job 36:21 applies to us as well as it applies to Job: *"Take care; do not turn to iniquity…"* Our natural default is not righteousness; we must *take care* to do what is right. What would it look like, practically, for you to *take care* to do what is right?

# • Day 80 •
Job 36:22–Job 37

*Pray.*

*Practice:*   Job 36:5 (NLT)—*"God is mighty, but He does not despise anyone! He is mighty in both power and understanding."*

*Read:*   Page 190–193 ("Elihu's Glorious Conclusion")

*Examine and Respond:*

1.  Having described how God speaks through affliction, Elihu now focuses on the majesty of God. Stedman states that this *"magnificent conclusion is a hymn to the glory of God"* (page 190). This "hymn" begins in Job 36:22. Write Job 36:22 in your own words as a prayer.

2.  In Job 36:24, we see one way in which we take care not to turn to iniquity, as Elihu just exhorted in verse 21. What does Elihu say we must remember to do in verse 24?

3.  How would you sum up Job 36:26–33? The thesis of this section could be seen as verse 26, with the rest of the chapter serving as an elaboration. What is Elihu saying here?

4.  Job 37 continues with powerful truths about God and our relation to Him.

    a. What are we supposed to do, according to Job 37:2?

    b. How does Job 37:5 answer our desire to understand everything?

    c. What are potential reasons given for the ways God works, according to Job 37:13?

    d. What good does it do us to heed Elihu's advice in Job 37:14 to *"stop and consider the wondrous works of God"*? How can this advice help us in any of life's hard (or good!) situations?

    e. Elihu is right to attribute full glory, majesty, and power to the Lord. However, it could be said that he takes it too far in Job 37:23, where he states, *"The Almighty—we cannot find Him."* The second part of Job 37:23 is absolutely true—that *"He is great in power; justice and abundant righteousness He will not violate"*—but is it true that *"we cannot find Him"*? Read Deuteronomy 4:29, Proverbs 8:17, Isaiah 55:6, Jeremiah 29:13, and Acts 17:27 for insight.

5.  Let us *"stop and consider the wondrous works of God"* (Job 37:14). To do so, read Psalm 104 aloud and take time to praise the Lord. He is worthy of every bit of our praise, and *He can be found!*

# • Day 81 •

Job 38:1–7

*Pray.*

*Practice:*   Isaiah 33:6—*"He will be the sure foundation for your times..."*

*Read:*   Page 195–197 (Chapter 12 Introduction and " 'Where Were You, Job?' ")

*Examine and Respond:*

1. Although Elihu had more help and truth to contribute than Job's other friends did, we breathe a universal sigh of relief knowing that we are finished reading from mortal man, and now God Himself will finally speak. We do not need to filter God's words to determine what is true!

   a. What does Proverbs 30:5 say about the truth of God's words?

   b. What effect does, or should, it have on you that God's words are true? What role does that play in your life? Look at the second part of Proverbs 30:5 for insight here.

2. In Job 38:1, God answers Job *"out of the whirlwind."* The Hebrew word for *"whirlwind"* can indicate a natural storm, but usually it is used in the context of God's supernatural appearances or actions. With that in mind, how would it be encouraging to Job (who has claimed that God does not intervene enough) that God comes to him in this way?

3. Look up Job 38:2 in a few different Bible versions, if possible.

   a. What does it mean to *"darken counsel by words without knowledge"* (ESV)?

   b. When are we prone to darken the light of God's message to us by our words?

4. a. What question does God ask Job in Job 38:4, and how is this question relevant to Job?

   b. When would it be helpful to ask yourself the same question? Fill in the blank with your own name: *Where were you, _____ , when God laid the foundation of the earth?*

5. Numerous Scriptures describe God's power over *"the foundations of the earth."* Read the following examples: 1 Samuel 2:8, 2 Samuel 22:16, Psalm 102:55, and Psalm 104:5.

6. It is an understatement to say that *foundations*—in Scripture, in engineering, in life—are crucial. What difference does, or should, it make in your life that as a child of God, *God* is your foundation? Look up Isaiah 28:16, Isaiah 33:6, and 1 Corinthians 3:11; then write a responsive prayer of thanks and trust.

# • Day 82 •
Job 38:8–18

*Pray.*

*Practice:*   Isaiah 33:6— *"He will be the sure foundation for your times..."*

*Read:*   Page 198–200 ("Mysteries of the Earth and Sea")

*Examine and Respond:*

1. In Job 38:8–11, God describes His power over what?

2. Where in Scripture do we see God's tangible power over the water? Read Matthew 8:23–27.

3. God displayed His power over water, too, when He first created it. Read Genesis 1:6–9. Is there anything you read in these verses today that you have not noticed before?

4. Where else in Scripture do we read of God's control over the sea? Examine these verses:

   a. Exodus 14:21–22—        b. Psalm 65:5–7—        c. Psalm 89:9—

   d. Psalm 107:29—           e. Jeremiah 5:22—       f. Jeremiah 31:35—

5. In Bible times, the ocean was seen as absolutely fearsome. Why do you think the Bible repeats so often that God has control over the sea?

6. In Job 38:12–15, God describes His power over what?

7. Read Genesis 1:1–5. What was the first thing on earth that God created?

8. God *commands* the light, and He *is* the source of all light. How do the Scriptures confirm this?
   a. Psalm 118:27—        b. 1 John 1:5—        c. Revelation 21:23—

9. God *created* light, God *is* the source of all light, and He has told us that *we* are now the light of the world! Write down what you read from Jesus in Matthew 5:14–16.

10. What conviction, encouragement, or inspiration did you receive from the verses you read today? Write down and pray for one difference you want these truths to make in your life.

# • Day 83 •
Job 38:19–38

*Pray.*

*Practice:* Isaiah 33:6—*"He will be the sure foundation for your times..."*

*Read:* Page 200–204 ("Mysteries of Light and Life" and "Mysteries of the Night Sky")

*Examine and Respond:*

1. How would you summarize in one sentence what God is communicating to Job in this section of Scripture (Job 38:19–28)?

2. Did you notice that when God finally speaks in the book of Job, He does not accuse Job of sin or blame Job as the cause of his own suffering, as Job's friends did? What does this show us about the character of God?

3. Complete the chart below to study this passage of Job in greater depth.

| *Verse in Job* | *Elsewhere in Scripture* | *For Further Thought* |
|---|---|---|
| Job 38:22— | Psalm 135:7— | What does it show you about God that He keeps unseen *"storehouses"* to use at later times? |
| Job 38:23— | Joshua 10:11—<br><br>Isaiah 30:30—<br><br>Revelation 16:21— | How does the fact that God tangibly intervenes in human history, using natural means such as hail, to punish His enemies and the enemies of His people encourage you or bolster your faith in Him? |
| Job 38:26— | Psalm 107:35— | These verses literally refer to geographic deserts; but how can they apply figuratively, too, to human lives—and thus encourage you? |
| Job 38:31–33— | Psalm 147:4—<br><br>Amos 5:8— | We are used to bowing our heads to pray, but Jesus literally *"lifted His eyes"* and *"looked to heaven"* (e.g., John 17:1) when He prayed. What can we learn about God by looking up to the skies? |

## • Day 84 •

Job 38:39–Job 39:30

*Pray.*

*Practice:*  Isaiah 33:6—*"He will be the sure foundation for your times..."*

*Read:*      Page 204–206 ("God Blesses the Beasts of the Wild")

*Examine and Respond:*

1. According to Stedman on page 204, *"In the last three verses of Job 38 and all of Job 39, God speaks to Job of His providential care for the animal world."* What do we learn about God's character when we reflect on the fact that He actually cares for animals?

2. The animals first mentioned in Job 38:39–41 are lions and ravens, which are both predators in the animal world—yet God tells Job that it is He who provides for these predators. We see, then, both a simplicity to God's provision and a complexity to it, as well. *Simplicity:* He is the one who provides. *Complexity:* By providing for the predators, He is giving up the life of their prey. How does this "simple yet complex" theme fit with the previous section, where God tries to get Job to understand that His ways are far beyond human understanding?

3. We know of people who lack basic needs. How can we reconcile this with God's provision?

4. Not every animal in Job 39 is listed as an example of God's provision. What point—about animals, humans, or Himself—does God make when He describes the following animals?

   a. Mountain goats (Job 39:1–4)          b. Wild donkey (Job 39:5–8)

   c. Wild ox (Job 39:9–12)                d. Ostrich (Job 39:13–18)

   e. Horse (Job 39:19–25)                 f. Hawk (Job 39:26–30)

5. Written all over the pages of Scripture are stories of God's provision. He is a, our, *the* Provider; it is in His very nature to provide. Read the following Scriptures about God's provision, jotting down any notes about these verses that you would like to remember.

   a. Genesis 9:3—                         b. Psalm 145:15–16—

   c. Matthew 6:25–30—                     d. Philippians 4:19—

# • Day 85 •
Job 40:1–5

*Pray.*

*Practice:* Isaiah 33:6—*"He will be the sure foundation for your times..."*

*Read:* Page 207–209 (" 'I Am Unworthy!' ")

*Examine and Respond:*

1. In Job 38–39, we saw that while God would have been justified in rebuking Job for some of what he has said about God, God simply asks Job, without condemning him, if he really knows what he is talking about. It seems as though all of God's words to Job have been intended to help Job redirect his focus off of what *seems to be* (his circumstances) to what *is* (the reality of God and His unfathomable ways).

   a. How would you summarize Job's response to God in Job 40:4–5?

   b. How does Job's response here differ from what he said in Job 31:37?

   c. What does this change in Job show about the effect God's words had on his perspective?

   d. God's words truly can and *do* change human perspective. In light of this fact, why is it important to be a diligent student of Scripture?

2. Rather than blaming Job for his suffering, God shows Job that the workings of the universe, our earth, and his life are beyond his understanding. How does John 9:1–3 relate to this?

3. A cursory reading of John 9:1–3 could easily lead to the thought, *"God is selfish and mean! Why would He make someone blind just to display His own works and glory?"* What we have hopefully learned from Job, however, is that that getting a glimpse of God's works and glory is worth much sacrifice—because to *see* more of God is to *know* more of God; to *know* Him more is to *love* Him more; to *love* Him more is to *trust* Him more; and to *trust* Him more is life-changing, soul-anchoring, hope-inducing, and worth the suffering it takes to get there. He is *always* working for a greater good, and glory awaits us.

   a. About what in your life can you look back on and reflect, *"This hard thing must have happened not because I sinned, but so the marvelous works of God could be displayed in my life!"* ?

   b. What we read in 2 Corinthians 4:17 could be illustrated with a balance scale, where one experience or condition far outweighs the other. Sketch the balance scale you would imagine when reading this verse. Thank the Lord that any suffering you endure as a child of God is never wasted. It is achieving good; it is worth it—even when it does not *feel* worth it at all!

# • Day 86 •
## Job 40:6–14

*Pray.*

*Practice:* Isaiah 33:6— *"He will be the sure foundation for your times..."*

*Read:* Page 211–213 (Chapter 13 Introduction and "It's Not Easy to Run the World")

*Examine and Respond:*

1. How would you define *repentance*?

2. When in your life did you come to an end and realize that you needed to turn 180° around?

3. God is the one who makes all things new; He is the God of new beginnings and fresh starts. How do we see this reality explained in Scripture?

   a. Ezekiel 36:26—                              b. Romans 6:4—

   c. Ephesians 4:24—                            d. Colossians 3:9–10—

   e. Revelation 21:5—

   f. How do these verses encourage you? How do they affect your view of how to live today?

4. a. Paraphrase God's words in Job 40:6–8. Eugene Peterson phrases them this way, in *The Message*: *"I have some more questions for you, and I want straight answers. Do you presume to tell me what I'm doing wrong? Are you calling me a sinner so you can be a saint?"*

   b. What do God's words in these verses show us about God's character and what He values?

5. On Day 43, we explored pride and humility—recurring themes throughout Scripture. How do God's words in Job 40:9–14 confirm that humility is of utmost importance to God?

6. Andrew Murray (1828–1917) exhorts us: *"Brethren, here is the path to the higher life. Down, lower down! Seek not, ask not for exaltation; that is God's work... and take no place before God or man but that of servant; that is your work; let that be your one purpose and prayer. God is faithful."* Let us take time today to pray earnestly for God to cultivate humility in our hearts—for only with humility can we see God and others with proper perspective. It matters.

# • Day 87 •
Job 40:15–41:9

*Pray.*

*Practice:* Isaiah 33:6—*"He will be the sure foundation for your times..."*

*Read:* Page 214–217 ("Behemoth and Leviathan")

*Examine and Respond:*

1. What does *behemoth* mean in Hebrew? What does *leviathan* mean?


2. a. What contrast is set up in Job 40:19?

   The behemoth _____ ,

   yet God _____ .


   b. What does this show us about the character and ability of God?


   c. How should this truth affect our daily lives?


3. Do you agree with Stedman that the beasts in this passage are symbolic? Why or why not?


4. Regardless of what exactly these beasts represent, what comfort and assurance can we have when we consider them in relation to God? Refer back to question 2 (Job 40:19).


5. Stedman notes on page 217 that Satan is behind a high-pressure attempt to make us *"conform and adopt the values and attitudes of the dying and fallen world around us."* How can we actively conform instead to the kingdom of God?

   a. Romans 12:2—


   b. 1 Peter 1:13–17—

# • Day 88 •
## Job 41:10–11

*Pray.*

*Practice:*   Isaiah 33:6—*"He will be the sure foundation for your times..."*

*Read:*   Page 217–219 ("The World, the Flesh, and the Devil")

*Examine and Respond:*

1.  On page 218, Stedman describes what could be thought of as *"Satan's unholy trinity."*

    a. What are the three forces Stedman lists that are at work for evil?

    b. Which of these three do you feel most powerfully at work in your life as a pull toward evil?

    c. Read Ephesians 6:12. What does Paul strongly assert as the root of our struggles?

    d. Now read that verse in its larger context: Ephesians 6:10–18. List all of the commands Paul gives us, the practical steps we can take to fight Satan and evil.

2.  Satan's ways are not new; from the beginning he has twisted and distorted what God has said.

    a. As you noted on Day 10, what does Satan ask Eve in Genesis 3:1?

    b. In your own life, when have you heard those whispers of doubt, *"Did God really say...?"* How did you fight these thoughts?

3.  As Stedman notes on page 219, *"God is in control of His universe... The world system is His problem, and He can handle it."* We cannot handle the world system—but God can. So let us echo the prayer of Daniel in Daniel 2 (MSG):

    > *Blessed be the name of God forever and ever,*
    > *He knows all, does all: He changes seasons and guides history.*
    > *He raises up kings and also brings them down...*
    > *He opens up the depths, tells secrets, sees in the dark—light spills out of Him!*
    > *God of all my ancestors, all thanks! all praise!*

# • Day 89 •
Job 41:12–34

*Pray.*

*Practice:*    Isaiah 33:6—*"He will be the sure foundation for your times..."*

*Read:*    Page 219–222 ("A Struggle Against Satanic Forces")

*Examine and Respond:*

1.    In this passage, we see Leviathan described in greater detail, and—in classic Satanic form, twisting and distorting what is good and true—he perversely copies God. Examine some parallels in the chart below.

| *Leviathan* | *God* |
|---|---|
| v. 14: The mouth of Leviathan is fearsome. | What comes out of the mouth of God? <br><br> Deuteronomy 8:3— <br><br> Matthew 4:4— |
| v. 15: Its closed-off shields protect its own back. | God "has our back"; He is our shield. <br><br> Proverbs 30:5— |
| v. 21: Its breath sets things on fire. | What does the breath of our Lord accomplish? <br><br> Genesis 2:7— <br><br> John 20:21–22— |
| v. 22: Its strength brings dismay. | What does God's strength provide for His children? <br><br> Psalm 28:7–8— |
| v. 33: Nothing on earth is its equal. | Leviathan was *created* by God! So he has not just an equal, but a superior. <br><br> Psalm 104:26— |
| v. 34: It is king over are those who are proud. | God's followers are those who are humble. <br><br> Isaiah 57:15— |

2.    Which aspect of God in the chart above do you feel the most grateful for in this season of your life? Take time to praise God and thank Him now. He is greater than all forces of evil and is worthy of all our praise.

## • Day 90 •
Job 42:1–6

*Pray.*

*Practice:*   Isaiah 33:6—*"He will be the sure foundation for your times..."*

*Read:*   Page 222–224 ("A Struggle Against Satanic Forces")

*Examine and Respond:*

1.  God has spoken; Job responds. Eugene Peterson phrases Job's reply to God like this: *"I'm convinced: You can do anything and everything. Nothing and no one can upset Your plans."*

    a. Write Job 42:1 in your own words.


    b. God's omnipotence (having *all power*) is on display from the very first pages of Scripture. How did God affirm the veracity of His omnipotence in Genesis 18:14?


    c. How is the truth of God's omnipotence echoed by Jesus in Matthew 19:26 and Mark 10:27?


    d. How can you apply Job 42:1 to a current situation in your life? The reality of God's omnipotence infuses every situation with hope.


2.  a. What does Job tell God in Job 42:3?


    b. How does it affect you that there truly are things *too wonderful for you to know*?


3.  In Job 42:5, Job makes a critical distinction between his prior knowledge of God and what he knows of God now.

    a. How would you describe this difference?


    b. Has a similar change occurred in your life? If so, what caused this shift?


4.  Can you relate to how Job feels in Job 42:6? How does Matthew 5:3–6 shed light on the value of feeling "poor in spirit"? *Blessed are those who mourn, for they will be comforted.* The comfort is not instantaneous—but it is sure.

# • Day 91 •
Job 42:7–8

*Pray.*

*Practice:*   Job 42:2—*"I know that You can do all things; no purpose of Yours can be thwarted."*

*Read:*   Page 225–227 (Chapter 14 Introduction and "A Distorted Image of God")

*Examine and Respond:*

1.  *Finally*, it seems, God calls Job's friends to account.

    a. What emotion does God acknowledge having in Job 42:7, and what can we learn from the fact that God has this emotion?

    b. In Job 42:7, what reason does God give for being angry with Job's three friends?

    c. Summarize the untruths about God that Job's friends espoused.

    d. When have you felt angry at someone else's failure to speak rightly about God?

2.  What do these verses indicate about prayer that is acceptable to God?

    a. Psalm 66:18–19—                    b. Proverbs 21:13—

    c. Proverbs 28:9—                       d. 1 John 3:21–22—

    e. In light of these truths, why do you think God asked Job to pray on his friends' behalf?

3.  God assures Job's friends in Job 42:8 that He will not give them the consequences they deserve. What insight does this provide about the character of God?

4.  What glaring irony do we see in God's mercy toward Job's friends, given their previous distortions of what God is like? (He definitely proves them wrong!)

5.  In Romans 8:31, what rhetorical question does Paul ask about God? How does this truth about God apply to God's defense of Job in Job 42:8? God is *for* His children, and *His* opinion is the one that matters.

# • Day 92 •
Job 42:7–8

*Pray.*

*Practice:*   Job 42:2—*"I know that You can do all things; no purpose of Yours can be thwarted."*

*Read:*   Page 227–229 ("A False Accusation Against Job")

*Examine and Respond:*

1. On page 228, Stedman provides a list of four things Job understood correctly when he talked to and about God. What did Job get right, and how can you imitate his example?

| *What Job Got Right* | *My "Take-Home"* |
|---|---|
| | |
| | |
| | |
| | |

2. Affirming the character of God through the deepest suffering—when the heart does not feel and the eyes do not see—is, as Stedman notes, *"the highest expression of faith."*

   a. Does this apply to anything you have experienced?

   b. How does this manifestation of faith relate to the description of faith in Hebrews 11:1?

3. God's requirement of sacrifice shows us that salvation depends on a substitute. *There is no other way.* Upon whose sacrifice do we depend, and how is this sacrifice described in Isaiah 53:12?

   Hymn-writer Elvina Hall sums it up this way: *"Jesus paid it all, all to Him I owe; Sin had left a crimson stain, He washed it white as snow."* Thank You, Jesus. We owe You everything.

# • Day 93 •
Job 42:8–10

*Pray.*

*Practice:* Job 42:2—*"I know that You can do all things; no purpose of Yours can be thwarted."*

*Read:* Page 229–231 ("The Power of Intercessory Prayer" and "Restoration and Renewal")

*Examine and Respond:*

1. *"God has not given us access through prayer so that we can bend His will to serve our own. Prayer is the way in which God enlists us in His plans and purposes,"* notes Stedman on page 229. What a gift it is to be able to be used by the Almighty God, who is perfectly capable of doing every good thing on His own! What do we learn in the following verses about intercessory prayer?

   a. Who intercedes for *us*, according to Romans 8:26?

   b. In Matthew 18:19–20, what do we learn about what happens when believers pray together?

   c. Are we supposed to pray primarily for other believers? See Matthew 5:44.

   d. According to James 5:16, how effective is intercessory prayer?

2. Job's willingness to pray for his accusatory friends—even before any of what he lost is restored—serves as an inspiring picture of what it looks like to *forgive*. What do we learn about forgiveness in the following verses?

   a. Matthew 6:14–15—

   b. Matthew 18:21–22—

   c. Luke 6:37—

   d. Luke 23:34—

   e. Ephesians 4:32—

   f. 1 Peter 3:9—

3. Read "Restoration and Renewal" on pages 230–231 of *Let God Be God* and use the space below to record any truths from this section that resonate with you most. Thank Him for His abundant love.

## • Day 94 •

Job 42:11

*Pray.*

*Practice:* Job 42:2—*"I know that You can do all things; no purpose of Yours can be thwarted."*

*Read:* Page 231–235 ("A Family Gathering" and "Using Our 'Baptized Imaginations' ")

*Examine and Respond:*

1. Scholars conjecture that Job is already about 70 years old at the time of his great suffering. Still, in Job 42:11, who comes to comfort him? What can we learn from this?

2. a. Although it is refreshing to read that Job is now surrounded by loved ones, where were they in Job 19:13?

   b. Does this change how you read Job 42:11?

   c. How do Job's family members either embody or fail to live up to the following verses?

   • Proverbs 19:6–7—                    • Proverbs 17:17—

3. What do Job's family members come to do for Job in Job 42:11? Use the "Blue Letter Bible" website to explore what could be meant by the original Hebrew of these verbs.

4. What are we to make of the phrase, *"the trouble the LORD had brought upon him"*?

5. Scholars explain that it was improper in the days of Job to approach any great man without bringing a present. How, then, must the gifts from Job's family members have been an encouragement to Job after all that he had endured?

6. After a time of unfathomable hardship, Job welcomes back his fair-weather family.

   a. What does this show us about Job?

   b. Would you have responded similarly?

   c. Which part of 1 Corinthians 13:5 best describes Job's love for his fellow man?

   d. What practical steps can *you* take to live out 1 Corinthians 13:5, like Job?

# • Day 95 •
Job 42:12–17

*Pray.*

*Practice:* Job 42:2—*"I know that You can do all things; no purpose of Yours can be thwarted."*

*Read:* Pages 235–238 ("Doubled Blessings" and "Peace, Fragrance, and Beauty")

*Examine and Respond:*

1. What does it show us about the character of God when we notice His *doubling* of everything Job had before his terrible suffering?

2. In Biblical times, names given to children often held great significance. It was also not as common to list women's names in historical recordings as men's.

   a. Why do you think Job's daughters are mentioned here by name?

   b. What symbolism, if any, do you notice in Job's daughters' names?

   | Name | Meaning in Hebrew | Potential Symbolism in the Context of Job |
   |---|---|---|
   | Jemima | "day by day" or "dove" | |
   | Kezia | "cassia," a cousin to cinnamon; used to sweeten foods | |
   | Keren-happuch | "horn of antimony" (a metal used for cosmetics/luxuries) | |

3. What does Job give his daughters (Job 42:15), and why is this noteworthy? What does it tell us about Job?

4. *"At the close of the story,"* notes Stedman on page 238, *"we see Job as a contented man—a man at peace with God, at peace with himself, and at peace with everyone around him. He has gone through a stormy time in his life, but God has sustained him and richly blessed him."* No one's life has a surprise ending; we all have to get out of here somehow! With the end in mind, what can you do now, today, to follow Job's example and take a step toward living in peace with God and others?

# • Day 96 •

*Pray.*

*Practice:* Job 42:2—*"I know that You can do all things; no purpose of Yours can be thwarted."*

*Read:* Pages 239–241 (Introduction to the Epilogue and "Trading Our Illusions for God's Truth")

*Examine and Respond:*

1. *Nec Aspera Terrent* is Latin for *Do not be terrified by adversity.* What have you studied in the book of Job about the character of God that can allow you not to be terrified by adversity?

2. We see the faithfulness of God in His sure and steady revelation of Himself and of salvation even in the earliest days of human history. What "illusions" did you once have about God that you now have come to realize are false, the longer you walk with Him?

3. *"The entire Bible, including the book of Job, challenges and corrects our false teaching"* (page 241). Scripture truly cleanses our minds.

   a. How does this truth fit with Romans 12:2?

   b. What role does your *mind* play in loving God? See Luke 10:27.

   c. What are some concrete ways to love God well with all of your mind?

4. In her book entitled *Loving God with All Your Mind*, Elizabeth George unpacks Philippians 4:8 as a key verse for Christians to focus on as we endeavor to love God with our minds. She notes: *"When you think on the powerful truths of Scripture, God uses His Word to change your way of thinking."* As noted on Day 46 of this study, we get to *choose* what we focus on. What will you choose to focus on today?

# • Day 97 •

*Pray.*

*Practice:*   Job 42:2—*"I know that You can do all things; no purpose of Yours can be thwarted."*

*Read:*   Pages 241–243 ("There is No Safe Place in War")

*Examine and Respond:*

1. Another highly recommended book written by Ray Stedman is *Spiritual Warfare: How to Stand Firm in the Faith.* Why would an entire book be devoted to this subject?

2. How important is this subject to you? How often do you think of the "cosmic battle plan" as you go through your daily life? Will you think of it more after studying the book of Job?

3. Let us revisit this key principle: *We are not on earth for fun.*

   a. How does this reality defy ways you tend to think, philosophies with which you grew up, and modes of living for everyone around us?

   b. How can you practically combat this way of thinking? What habits of thought or action can you put in place to keep unseen reality at the forefront of your mind and life?

   c. Stedman notes that we are on earth to live out a deeper and larger purpose. How would you describe that purpose?

   d. Do you agree with Solomon's statement in Ecclesiastes 12:13? Write out the verse in the space below, along with your corresponding thoughts.

   e. How does Mark 12:30–31 align with what God's purpose is for your life? What steps can you take to align your life to this purpose more intentionally?

# • Day 98 •

*Pray.*

*Practice:* Job 42:2—*"I know that You can do all things; no purpose of Yours can be thwarted."*

*Read:* Pages 243–245 ("The True Nature of Faith" and "The True Nature of Fallen Humanity")

*Examine and Respond:*

1. Our faith is proven in hard times. How does 1 Peter 1:6–7 confirm this truth?

2. How is praying for our suffering to be removed, while simultaneously entrusting the situation ultimately to God *("not my will, but Thine be done")*, an act of *faith*?

3. God refers to Job as *"my servant Job."*

    a. What does this show us about God?

    b. What does this show us about Job?

    c. Are you content to be God's *servant*?

4. How does Matthew 20:26–28 illuminate the idea of servanthood?

5. How does it help you to know that Jesus Christ Himself was called the Father's servant?

6. Stedman points out the universal human desire to *"possess some of the glory that is due to God alone"*—essentially, we want others to praise us. *But this is not good for us*—and trials help burn it out. Are *any* created things supposed to be worshiped? Read Revelation 19:10 and Revelation 22:9 for insight.

7. In 1 Timothy 1:17, Paul sums up the glory that is due to God alone. Write out this verse in the space below and pray it aloud to the only one deserving of our praise.

# • Day 99 •

*Pray.*

*Practice:*   Job 42:2—*"I know that You can do all things; no purpose of Yours can be thwarted."*

*Read:*   Pages 245–247 ("Why We Suffer")

*Examine and Respond:*

1.  How does the life of Christ display the fact that sometimes we suffer for no other reason than that *"our affliction accomplishes God's purposes"* (page 245)?

2.  If our suffering lies within the greater purpose of God, can any effort on our part prevent that suffering? Examine this idea in the verses below.

    a. Job 42:2—

    b. Proverbs 19:21—

    c. Isaiah 14:27—

    d. Isaiah 46:10—

3.  If, as the verses above confirm, we cannot prevent the suffering that lies within the purposes of God for us, what should our approach to inevitable suffering be instead?

4.  *"It is a high and holy privilege,"* notes Stedman, *"to uphold the glory of God against the accusations of the devil. If we will learn to see our sufferings in light of the spiritual war that has been raging since before the creation of the human race, it will transform our lives and our pain. It will awaken us to the high and holy privilege of sharing in the sufferings of our Lord Jesus Christ."*

    How can we come closer to embracing this view—to see our sufferings as a *privilege*? What will it take from us?

5.  In the space below, draw a sketch of what it might look like to see life *"from the long view of eternity"* (page 247).

# • Day 100 •

*Practice:*   Job 42:2—*"I know that You can do all things; no purpose of Yours can be thwarted."*

*Read:*        Pages 247–249 ("The Character of God")

*Examine and Respond:*

1.  Why do you think Stedman ends his book with *The Character of God*?

2.  In what ways would it be fitting for the book of your own life to conclude with its final chapter centering on the character of God?

3.  What does Stedman write in this chapter that resonates most with you? What truths do you want to tuck away for the times of deep suffering that, if they are not already here, will inevitably come your way?

4.  A wise and beloved pastor, Old Testament scholar Glen Snyder, captures the essential question of the book of Job this way:

    "IS GOD ENOUGH?"

    Job emerges from the depths of suffering with the firm conviction that indeed, God *is* enough. May the fires of trial that come our way work this purifying and redeeming work in us, too; and may we reach the other side of hardship with full assurance, anchored hope, and abounding joy, declaring with Job:

    "TRULY, GOD IS ENOUGH.
    *And He was* with *me in that fire."*

    As we endure the suffering that is necessary to lead us to that life-altering assurance, let us imagine Job, cheering for us earnestly from the other side:

    *"My dear brothers and sisters!*
    **It is worth it all.***"*

*Lord, help us to trust You more and to suffer well.*

*You are all we need.*

*In the precious name of Jesus Christ,*
*our Redeemer Who Lives,*
*our One and Only Hope,*
*whose name we bear*
*in the hour of affliction,*

*Amen.*